PRIMARY

PROFESSIONAL BOOKSHELF

HOW TO TEACH READING

a balanced approach

CHICHESTER INST
HIGHER EDUCATIO
AUTHOR
BIELBY
D0302342
TITLE
HOW
372.4
DEC98 TES

NICHOLAS BIELBY

© 1998 Nicholas Bielby

Published by Scholastic Ltd
Villiers House
Clarendon Avenue
Leamington Spa
Warwickshire CV32 5PR

Author Nicholas Bielby
Editor Nancy Terry
Assistant Editor Irene Goodacre
Series Designer Lynne Joesbury
Designer Mark Udall

1 2 3 4 5 6 7 8 9 0 8 9 0 1 2 3 4 5 6
Designed using Adobe Pagemaker

The right of Nicholas Bielby to be identified as the Author of this Work has been asserted by him in accordance with the Copyright, Designs and Patents Act 1988.

DEDICATION

For Isabella Morwenna Elsdon Howey, who was born on the day I finally sent off the manuscript for this book.
I would like to thank my cousin, Jonathan Bielby, of Wakefield Cathedral, for transcribing the music for the alphabet chant.

British Library Cataloguing-in-Publication Data
A catalogue record for this book is available from the British Library.

ISBN 0-590-53887-X

All rights reserved. This book is sold subject to the condition that it shall not, by way of trade or otherwise, be lent, hired out or otherwise circulated without the publisher's prior consent in any form of binding or cover other than that in which it is published and without a similar condition, including this condition, being imposed upon the subsequent publisher.

No part of this publication may be reproduced, stored in a retrieval system, or transmitted, in any form or by any means, electronic, mechanical or otherwise, without the prior permission of the publisher.

ACKNOWLEDGEMENTS

© Material from the National Curriculum is Crown copyright and is reproduced by permission of the Controller of HMSO, 1995.
Barrie Wade and **Maggie Moore** for the use of adapted text from *No Worries* Collins Pathways Series © Barrie Wade and Maggie Moore (Collins Educational).

PRIMARY
PROFESSIONAL BOOKSHELF

CONTENTS

PRIMARY
PROFESSIONAL BOOKSHELF

INTRODUCTION

This book is designed to help you to teach reading. But it is not solely, or even primarily, a recipe book. It is a book about diet – with some recipes thrown in. It discusses the essential nutrients for learning to read and how they may be combined to constitute a balanced diet.

In the last few years, a broad consensus has developed among reading researchers and experts about how children learn to read. As a result, some of the old battle lines, such as that between the competing orthodoxies of the language experience approach and traditional phonics, should now be left behind. The positive elements of both these orthodoxies find their place in a balanced approach based on current knowledge about how children learn to read.

This book, then, aims to offer a balanced view of how reading should be taught in the light of the current academic consensus and within the framework prescribed by the National Curriculum and the National Literacy Strategy.

Although a theoretical model of reading development is not spelled out in either the National Curriculum or the National Literacy Strategy's *Framework for Teaching*, both are informed by contemporary research findings. For example, the language of 'balance' and of 'phonological awareness', 'phonic' and 'graphic knowledge' and 'contextual understanding' in the National Curriculum is evidence of this. If, as teachers, we want to develop our own balanced, professional view and be in a better position to interpret and implement the statutory requirements intelligently, we need to understand the model of reading development that underlies them and what research tells us about learning and teaching.

This book looks at the elements identified as contributing to the reading process and suggests how they can best be taught in a balanced way, so that they meld in the child's ability to read and comprehend written text. It discusses these in terms of practical activities you can do with children in the classroom.

HOW THE BOOK IS ORGANIZED

The book is divided into five sections:

Part One: Introduction discusses the notion of 'balance' and sketches the current theoretical model of the reading processes and how children learn to read.

The following three sections look at the development of reading skills.

Part Two: Sounds and Symbols deals with the sounds of the language, teaching the alphabet and a first sight vocabulary, and the beginnings of mapping sounds onto letters and spellings.

Part Three: Working Out Words examines the various ways we try to identify words, learning to work them out from their spellings and recognize them as sight vocabulary.

Part Four: Constructing Meaning discusses the processes by which we put words together to make sense and interpret texts to achieve comprehension.

Each chapter in Part Two, Part Three and Part Four, then, presents an aspect of reading theory and suggests ways of teaching the relevant skills.

Finally, *Part Five: Developing Strategies* considers the practical aspects of teaching – how to assess and develop children's skills while listening to them read; and how to orchestrate balanced classroom teaching strategies within the overall parameters of the National Curriculum and National Literacy Strategy.

BALANCE

What is meant by a 'balanced approach' to teaching reading? Successful reading is a complex of skills that works in an apparently seamless way. This seamlessness depends upon balancing various contributory elements in such a way that they mutually support, correct and reinforce each other. This is the balance in children's reading strategies that we, as teachers, must try to promote by teaching in a balanced way. Whatever skills we are teaching, we must do it in a way that leads to balanced and integrated development.

THE THREE SOURCES OF INFORMATION

It is generally agreed that, as we read, we bring together information from three different sources:

✧ from the printed words on the page (obviously!);

✧ from our implicit grammatical knowledge and expectations about how words link together within and between sentences to make sense;

✧ from our sense of meaning – based both on our general knowledge of what is probable or possible in the real world and in stories and, more immediately, on our developing grasp of the meaning of a sentence or passage as we proceed through it.

Let's consider some examples of what these three points might mean. First, of course, reading means reading the words on the page. The infant who holds a book and recites the story from memory without looking at the text is not reading, only 'pretend reading'. But what this activity demonstrates is that the child knows what reading is meant to accomplish – getting specific words from print. The child is unlikely to recite, or 'pretend read' the story in the absence of the text. Reading-for-real means deliberately looking at the text to extract its wording, not some remembered or invented wording.

Secondly, an example of the influence of grammatical knowledge. Lee reads:

> Then he would set the nets again.

where the text actually says:

> Then he would set his nets again.

Not an important misreading, perhaps, but nevertheless a misreading. But significantly what Lee says is grammatically correct. And further, the word 'the' also correctly refers back to the fact that the nets have been mentioned earlier in the text – they are the same nets, not some other nets. Lee has a drive, shared with all children from the first few months of learning to read, to produce sentences that make sense grammatically. Experts as diverse as Marie Clay and Ken Goodman see this propensity to seek grammatical coherence as a vital element in learning to read. Lee implicitly anticipates that a noun phrase will follow the verb, and 'the' is an obvious introductory word for a noun phrase. In Lee's case, his grammatical expectation dominates at the expense of the information he should have derived from the printed page. His grammatical expectation does not *support*, but *replaces* recognition of the printed word. The textual and grammatical sources of information are not in balance.

Thirdly, an example of the influence of the developing sense of meaning in a passage. A child reads:

> The terrible, terrible tiger... jumped on me.

where the text actually says:

> That terrible, terrible tiger... leapt on me.

We shall return to this example, but suffice to say at this point the child anticipates the meaning at the expense of reading the actual text accurately. The child is involved in *making* the meaning, and is not just a *consumer* of meaning. Such involvement in constructing meaning is invaluable for comprehension *if* it comes under the control of the written text – but not if it is used to replace or dispense with the text.

Reading depends not only on our *reacting* to the print on the page but also on our *anticipating and seeking* meaning from the text: not just on what we get from the text, but also on what we bring to the text. Indeed, the different theories about how to teach reading differ primarily in terms of what the theorists think more important – the decoding of the printed text or the meaning-making we bring to it.

TWO KINDS OF IMBALANCE

Let's look at some examples of how over-stressing the importance of one or other of these aspects can upset the balance.

First, the lack of balance which can result from meaning-centred approaches. Redfern and Edwards (1992) argue that reading isn't simply a mechanical process of 'cracking the code' as traditional phonics and look-and-say approaches seem to suggest. Instead, they argue:

> ...in order to make sense of print, we make intelligent guesses. We use our experience of language and life, and our knowledge of the way that stories work to help us.
>
> (page 4)

This is the 'language experience' approach. They argue that, in relation to the 'terrible, terrible tiger' example given earlier, the child shouldn't be corrected, since the story makes sense and that this kind of 'miscue' (mistake) will gradually disappear with more experience.

What is not explained is *why* it will disappear. Presumably, at some point, the intelligent guess will be displaced by actually attending to what is written. Presumably, at some point in the future, this will occur spontaneously. But of course, the teacher can intervene to help it occur sooner rather than later. It is possible, for example, at the end of the page, to ask the child if she thinks she might have read something incorrectly. You don't have to interrupt the flow of the story to invite the child to focus on the wording and reflect upon the accuracy of her performance. You might say, 'Yes, you really got the meaning there. It was exciting, wasn't it? But did you read every word correctly? Where do you think you didn't get it quite right?'

It is not good enough to suggest, by *not* drawing attention to the actual wording, that guessing is satisfactory. In the long run, guessing is a dead end strategy. It is much better to encourage the child to monitor her own performance for accuracy, as well as meaning.

For our second example, by contrast we can look at *Reading Fever: Why phonics must come first* (Turner and Burkard, 1996). The authors explicitly reject a balanced approach. They castigate language experience approaches that place meaning at the centre of the enterprise, saying they are based upon 'hallucination rather than evidence'. They equate expecting children to read books before they have mastered the alphabet with asking children to add or subtract before they can count to ten. They argue that:

> The use of reading schemes and real books should be encouraged only when basic phonetic skills are established and when reading practice is desired.
>
> (TES 6/12/96)

That is, phonic skills have to be established before children can be allowed to encounter the very books that might motivate them to learn to read and which might build on children's existing but fragmentary and unformalised experience and knowledge of print. Turner and Burkard believe children must not be encouraged to exploit their capacity to learn and recognize a sight vocabulary of whole words before learning their letters.

What Turner and Burkard demonstrate is the classic phonics-first approach that tends to see children as empty pitchers to be filled with phonic knowledge and programmed with procedures, not as people with pre-existing language and literacy experience which they can use intelligently and imaginatively to help solve the problem of print. Their model phonics learner is a passive recipient of information and procedures, not an active participant in the learning process.

THE IMPORTANCE OF PHONICS

To criticize the phonics-first approach is not to discount the importance of phonic knowledge or phonic strategies. Phonics is an essential nutrient in a balanced diet. And traditional phonics can undoubtedly be a literacy life-saver when dealing with exceptional children, for instance Down's Syndrome and dyslexics, whom other approaches have failed. But even if, in teaching today, 'phonics is the missing ingredient' (McNee, 1996), we should not treat it as the whole diet.

Nevertheless, teaching the alphabet and phonics early is important and should be a way to help children make sense of the sight vocabulary that they are learning at the same time. This way, they can use its lessons for developing their own word attack strategies. They should be helped to use phonic knowledge, knowledge of spelling patterns and whole-word knowledge in combination with their intelligent anticipation of likely meaning in order to come to a meaningful and accurate reading of the text. A balanced approach means having a flexible array of strategies available to tackle texts and using these strategies in concert.

BALANCED TEACHING

What a balanced approach to teaching reading does is recognize the importance of all three sources of information available to the reader – the grammatical context, the meaning context and the text itself. It exploits them all in such a way that they mutually interact with and support each other in the reading process. An essential element in balanced reading development is the integration, coordination or orchestration of these different sources of information in a system concerned with both meaning and accuracy.

Markers of balanced development in the beginning reader include refusing to guess, slowing down and studying difficult words (perhaps sounding them aloud or silently mouthing them) and self-correcting after a miscue. While Redfern and Edwards are happy with miscues that don't change the meaning (as in the 'terrible tiger' example given earlier), the child who is developing in a balanced way will not be happy when there is any sort of mismatch between what she reads and the writing on the page. Miscues like 'jumped' for 'leapt' will only disappear if the child is habitually cross-checking between all three sources of information in order to arrive at an accurate and meaningful reading of the text. This interaction between the sources of information shows itself in the child's self-monitoring and self-correction which thereby act as a self-tutoring mechanism.

A balanced approach to *teaching* reading will not replace but will add to the prompting strategies suggested by Redfern and Edwards. They suggest that the teacher can help children by:

- pointing to the picture, if it is relevant;

✧ asking a question to remind them of the context, for example, 'Where did they say they were going?';
✧ re-reading the sentence with expression up to the unknown word to remind them of the context;
✧ saying or pointing to the first letter of the word;
✧ covering part of the word to make it easier to recognize;
✧ telling the child the word in order to avoid losing momentum.

Additionally, a more balanced approach would include encouraging the child to:

✧ study the spelling of a new word to look for any familiar patterns;
✧ sound out the letters and blend the sounds where appropriate (ie, where the spelling is phonically regular);
✧ study the spelling of a new word to remember it in the future;
✧ identify, on looking back over a page, what words were misread or were difficult and say what the problems were;
✧ check that the word she expects to come next corresponds with the word on the page;
✧ be alert to whether the word she is reading makes sense in context, and self-correct as appropriate;
✧ respond appropriately to, 'Does it actually say that?' or 'Does that make sense?' by reviewing the text more carefully.

This is a not an exhaustive list, but what you will notice about these additional prompts is that they suggest strategies either for word attack or self-monitoring. In each case, they encourage strategies that empower the child by giving her a sense that she is potentially in control of her own reading.

BALANCING THE SOURCES OF INFORMATION

The balance that we should be encouraging in the child is one in which the three sources of information – the print on the page, grammar and meaning – all play their part. But the print on the page plays the leading role. It is where reading starts from, and it is the final arbiter of what is being said.

The way the three sources of information interact with each other is crucial. If the child anticipates what comes next, then the printed word will either confirm or disconfirm the guess and, if disconfirmed, the reader should self-correct appropriately. If the child half reads and half guesses, both the printed text and the context of meaning provide corrective cross-checks against each other. If the child correctly identifies the printed word, the context of meaning both confirms the reading and is confirmed and developed by it. If the child misidentifies a word and the sentence does not make sense, any anomaly of meaning should prompt the child to review the text and self-correct.

At its best, the interaction between the sources of information operates in the following way: decoding the print takes the leading role, but may be supported where the context of meaning primes the reader's expectancy, facilitating both word identification and comprehension. The overall coherence of grammar and meaning confirm the reading, and the reading extends the overall meaning. The aim of balanced teaching is to work towards this pattern of interaction as its goal.

CONCLUSION

Contemporary reading research has taught us a great deal about how children learn to read. Experts recognize the importance of a proper balance between children's reading strategies to allow successful development to take place. Balanced strategic development is attainable through balanced teaching and balanced teaching is dependent on the teacher understanding the processes of reading development. The next chapter will explore the processes and development of reading in more detail in order to provide the conceptual underpinning for the approach taken to teaching in the rest of the book.

Note: I have indicated the *sound* (as distinct from the visual identity) of a word or letter by putting it between slashes thus: 'cat' is pronounced /cat/. I have also adopted the convention of referring to the child as 'she' throughout.

CHAPTER 1

THE READING PROCESS

Before we try to teach reading, it is useful to know something about how reading works – about how adults do it, and about how children learn to do it. We want to make sure that how we teach supports how children learn.

As well as learning from research, we can learn quite a lot from inspecting our own reading processes. If we recognize the processes in ourselves, we are more likely to be intelligently sensitive to their development in children. Consequently, before looking at the research, this chapter will begin by looking at ourselves.

LEARNING FROM OUR OWN MISTAKES

Fortunately, I am not very good at reading! I read slowly and I tend to hear what I read very clearly in my mind's ear (which, perhaps, explains why I like poetry so much). And I make mistakes. I am specially interested in the mistakes because of what they tell me about my reading processes.

By 'reading processes', I mean what takes place between looking at a page of print and understanding it. It involves all the processes of perception and interpretation that go on in my head. Let's look at two reading errors I made recently to see what we can learn from them.

ERROR 1

The other day I misread the word 'embed'. I read it as /emb'd/, and I didn't know what it meant. I had to go back and re-read it. So what had been going on?

✧ I didn't recognize the word as a whole, sight-vocabulary word that I knew or I would have got it right straightaway.

✧ I can't have processed the word phonically, letter-by-letter, because the word itself is phonically regular, and if I had processed it phonically, there should have been no problems.

✧ I 'heard' a word in my mind's ear which I didn't recognize.

✧ I have an instant monitoring system that virtually automatically makes me re-read anything that doesn't make sense.

I believe the explanation for the misreading is as follows. The grammar of the sentence I read led me to anticipate that a verb would follow. When I saw the '-ed' at the end of the word, I interpreted it as the past tense ending. That is, I processed the word as 'emb + ed' (and not as 'em + bed') and I pronounced it (in my head) accordingly. At some level – perhaps at the level of identifying spelling chunks or perhaps at the level of monitoring internalized pronunciation – I realized I didn't recognize the word. This failure of meaning caused the self-correction strategy (review and reprocessing) to kick in. Clearly, a different processing strategy then correctly identified the word.

If this is what happened, it suggests that the processing system is flexible. It does not, necessarily, work in terms of whole words or letter-by-letter recognition, but can work by finding familiar (pronounceable and/or meaningful) spelling chunks in words, in order to reconstruct and identify them.

This characteristic of reading is also evident amongst children learning to read. Bussis *et al* (1985) noted that as children progressed in reading skills, most of them came to recognize the spelling and grammatical meaning of frequently encountered word-parts – the affixes at the beginnings and ends of words, like 'un-', 'pre-', '-tion', '-ful', '-ed'. The children seemed to construct a vocabulary of 'sight affixes' in much the same way as they had constructed a vocabulary of 'sight-words' at an earlier stage of reading.

So my error in reading '-ed' as the past tense of a verb was based on skills I probably learned quite early on in my reading. These skills include: knowing when to anticipate a verb in a sentence; recognizing '-ed' as a chunk; pronouncing it after a 'b' as /'d/ and not /ed/ (as in 'rubbed', 'combed'). These are highly functional skills that I had occasion to notice only when they gave rise to a mistake.

What we should learn from errors like this is:

- while skilled readers sometimes identify words whole, sometimes they identify words by reconstructing them from their constituent spelling chunks;
- children should be encouraged to identify affixes and to see complex words as consisting of meaningful spelling chunks.

After all, this is exactly what the National Curriculum is encouraging in talking about 'graphic knowledge' – a theme to which we will return in Chapter 8.

ERROR 2

Recently I read the following phrase, 'In the year 1880s', only to realize it didn't make sense. On re-reading the phrase, I discovered it actually said, 'In the early 1880s'.

The immediate points that strike me about this misreading are:

- all the letters of 'year' appear in 'early';
- the spelling sequence 'ear' appears in both words;
- for many of us, there is no distinction in pronunciation between 'the ear(ly)' and 'the year';
- the expression '1880' refers to a year, so seeing it coming may have primed me to expect the word 'year'.

The error would appear to be explained by the coincidence of anticipated meaning with certain spelling elements (and, possibly, coincidences of pronunciation). The reading process does not just *respond* to spellings, but *seeks* them in the light of expectations – even to the extent, sometimes, of making them up! Perception seems to be trying to match the visual input with known spelling patterns, and if one doesn't pay close enough attention to the print on the page, it is possible for a mismatch to be made. In this case, the context seems to have facilitated the mismatch.

As with the first example, when an anomaly in meaning was detected, my self-correction system required me to re-read the text. Automatic self-correction is an important function in reading. This is why the National Curriculum on Reading at Key Stage 1 says that children, '... should be taught to keep the overall sense of a passage in mind *as a checking device*' (my italics).

EXPECTATIONS AND PRIMING

As adult readers, we generally process the print on the page more swiftly than we anticipate or construct meaning. But it is meaning that confirms that we have read something successfully and, if we don't find meaning, we will review the text. Children, on the other hand, tend to process the print more slowly than they can anticipate the meaning and, consequently, make more errors based on anticipation, reading what they expect the text to say.

Meaning can prime the visual recognition system with expectations. Hence we identify words more quickly if they have been recently activated, if their meanings relate to the current context and if the words relate to our own personal interests – as when I read the small ads heading *Pets' Corner* as saying *Poets' Corner*! This process of priming can lead to the misidentification of words – though more usually what it does is to speed up correct identification.

CHARACTERISTICS OF THE READING PROCESS

What we have said so far suggests certain characteristics of the reading process, and a large body of research evidence confirms these suggestions (see Bielby (1994) for further discussion). We may summarize them thus:

✧ the processing of spellings involves seeking familiar and meaningful 'chunks' or spelling sequences;

✧ internalized pronunciation plays a part in the reading process;

✧ 'bottom up' information derived from the print on the page and 'top down' information derived from grammar and meaning,

and leading to anticipation, play interactive roles in the process;
✧ reading is not just a mechanical translation of print into words, but is an active search for meaning based on this interactive processing of the print;
✧ this quest for meaning goes on at every level, from seeking known letter-shapes and spelling sequences, to anticipating the flow of grammar and meaning; from checking spelling patterns for pronounceability and meaning to checking the sentences for grammatical and semantic coherence.

STAGES OF READING DEVELOPMENT

What we have said so far is largely concerned with the adult reading process. But children have to learn to read and they can't learn all the adult skills at one go. Adult reading is an orchestrated complex of skills – skills that interact with each other so effortlessly that we are largely unconscious of them, just as the millipede doesn't have to think which leg to move first!

The child, however, has to learn the various skills, sometimes consciously and very deliberately, sometimes more subliminally, and has to learn to coordinate them. We can see something of the complexity of this process if we 'unpack' what is meant by the term 'sight vocabulary'.

As adults, we recognize instantly nearly all the words we read without having to think about how we do it. We have a huge sight vocabulary and reading development is largely a matter of developing it further. But developing it has two aspects: increasing the number of words and learning more efficient ways to identify words more or less instantaneously.

The notion of a sight vocabulary is much more complex than is commonly realized. As adults, we read relatively quickly because our extensive sight vocabulary precludes our having to work out words by more laborious means. The child's first reading vocabulary is also a sight vocabulary, yet it is very different from that of an adult – in quality as well as quantity. Adults read words without working them out because they have worked them out and learned them at some time in the past. The child's first sight vocabulary is not worked out at all but is simply remembered rote-fashion from some detail.

The key question is, *how* do you recognize the words of your sight vocabulary? With initial learners, the process is relatively unsophisticated; with adults, it is very sophisticated, though apparently effortless and largely unconscious. The development from one to the other can be seen as a series of stages or phases (see Ehri (1995)).

STAGE 1: PRE-ALPHABETIC SIGHT VOCABULARY

Virtually all pre-readers possess at least a small vocabulary of 'sight-words' that they can reliably identify in their normal context, if not out of context. The child may learn to recognize her name from the plaque on the bedroom door, 'McDonald's' from its distinctive 'M', and the words 'No smoking' from a sign. For such a pre-alphabetic sight vocabulary to work, the child does not need to know the alphabet, the sound values of the letters, or even in which direction to process print. She simply needs to be told and to remember.

Such pre-alphabetic processes are not foolproof. The child may know the word in one context and not another because, in effect, she 'reads' the context rather than the word. The child may infer the brand name 'Ivory' says 'soap' because it is printed on a soap wrapper!

Children tend to identify their pre-alphabetic sight-words from some detail that catches their attention. Typically, but not necessarily, such details will involve letters – for instance, Seymour and Elder (1985) cite one boy who identified any word with 'k' in it as 'black'; Stuart (1995) cites a girl who identified a word with an 'a' in it as 'Christina' – presumably because 'a' is a salient letter in her own name! But other characteristics, such as word length, may also be important.

We often exploit this spontaneous propensity, encouraging children to learn the first words of a reading scheme using flash cards or little boxes of word-cards to take home, so that they can experience initial success in tackling their first books. But we don't know *how* they are learning the words. Each child will latch on to a different detail.

This detail, however, may not be one that opens up the way to better reading. The boy who knew the word 'television' 'because of the dots' hasn't grasped onto anything that will help him in the long run. Some experts are reluctant to call pre-alphabetic sight reading 'reading' at all because it does not depend upon understanding the nature of print and the significance of the alphabet. But in controlled situations it can be useful in developing reading and giving children confidence.

However, the pre-alphabetic processes do not have much mileage in them. Stuart (1995) notes one limitation:

> One of the first things children do is learn which words they are learning to recognise in print. (page 49)

Children tend to think that they are only meant to read the words they are being taught and don't attempt or learn any others.

A further limitation is that, as the vocabulary increases, the process becomes less reliable, and it will not readily expand beyond a limited number of words – too many words that have a 'k' in them don't say 'black'!

A third major limitation of pre-alphabetic reading is that it doesn't provide any way of dealing with new words and children have to revert to guessing. Nor do they have a visual way of checking a false identification, so self-correction is negligible. Reliance on a pre-alphabetic sight vocabulary and guessing is the mark of an early, or struggling reader.

EARLY ERROR TYPES

Stuart (1995) distinguishes five different levels of word identification error she found in children during their first eighteen months in school. Three of these levels fall within the pre-alphabetic reading phase. They represent different levels of responding analytically to the letters in a word:

1. When there is little visual resemblance to the target word – perhaps a single shared letter, for example, reading 'hat' as 'John'.

The children who make most errors of this kind and who persist with them longest, are typically the children who know least about letter names and letter sounds. As such, they are the children with the least idea how to look at a word.

2. When more than one letter is shared, for example, reading 'can' as 'and', 'home' as 'shop'.

No regard is given to the order of the letters in the word. By the end of the first year in school, only struggling readers with poor letter knowledge are making such errors.

3. When the final letters are shared with the target word, for example, reading 'green' as 'open'.

Again, persistence in such errors relates to a low reading age.

We will consider levels 4 and 5, under the next stage, partial alphabetic reading, as it is possible that phonological factors, as well as visual factors, play a part.

STAGE 2: PARTIAL ALPHABETIC READING

When children start to learn the alphabet and the sound values of the letters, partial alphabetic reading becomes possible. This stage is an obvious development from the pre-alphabetic-cum-guessing stage. Being alerted to letters and their sounds, the child uses partial phonic cues, typically initial letter sounds, to prompt recognition or guessing. As teachers we often encourage this explicitly, saying 'Sound the first letter'.

Levels 4 and 5 of Stuart's (1995) categorization of errors correspond with this stage:

4. When initial letters are shared with the target word, for example, reading 'just' as 'jelly', 'sound' as 'some'.

These errors are the most common and their prevalence doesn't relate to reading age. While clearly these errors *are* errors, they are also markers of development, of moving towards alphabetic reading. Halfway through their first year at school, those children who knew most letter *names* were making most errors of this kind. By the beginning of the second year, it was the children who knew most letter *sounds* who made most of these errors. Stuart notes:

> This may reflect the fact that it is possible to use the first letter either as a visual cue or as a phonological cue. (page 51)

5. When initial and final letters are shared with the target word, for example, reading 'guess' as 'grass', 'driver' as 'dinner'.

Within the first eighteen months at school, it is the children with the highest reading ages and most developed letter name and sound knowledge who make most errors of this kind – that is, make the most *attempts* to use complex alphabetic cues in reading. It could be said that these are the children with the clearest internalized visual representation of the words, the clearest mental templates. At the same time, they are the children best equipped to use phonological knowledge in word identification. This is because mapping the phonological and spelling patterns onto each other mutually clarifies and reinforces both.

Stuart categorized errors of types 1, 2 and 3 as 'bad' because they could not easily lead on to a correct mapping of sounds onto letters. Types 4 and 5, however, she considered 'good' because they could lead on to such a correct mapping. Over her longitudinal study she looked at the balance between 'good' and 'bad' errors and, particularly, she looked for the point, for each child, at which 'good' errors outnumbered 'bad'. She found that once the balance changed, it changed permanently, and that this point of change occurred when the child was not only phonologically aware, but also knew the sounds for at least thirteen letters. She cites the example of Martha who read 'gun' as 'garden' but added the comment, 'You didn't write enough letters.' Stuart remarks:

> It looked as though knowing about the sounds in spoken words, and knowing about how letters related to those sounds, guided the way children looked at and tried to remember printed words. (page 53)

What she is discussing here is how mapping begins, building up a mental template or internalized representation of a word.

Partial alphabetic reading not only helps to prompt guesses with phonetic cues but it also enables children to remember new words. There are now phonetic cues to support memory. At the same time, it strengthens children's grasp on the words they learned as pre-alphabetic sight-words. Learning to discriminate letters focuses children's attention on the constituent letters as the relevant details of the words they already know, and enables them to discover phonetic cues to help their identification.

Partial alphabetic reading depends on the coming together of two elements: phonological awareness and alphabetic knowledge. Phonological awareness permits children to perceive shared sounds in different words. Alphabetic knowledge includes the visual discrimination of letters and learning the letter sounds. Seeing letters as the visual equivalent of the heard similarities between words opens a whole new chapter of reading skills.

STAGE 3: FULL ALPHABETIC READING

Full alphabetic reading involves the child in processing all the letters in sequence. This may mean traditional phonics – the synthetic phonic processes of sounding out and blending the individual letters and digraphs – but it also means more than this. Children will start to make their own links between spellings and pronunciations. Frequently encountered spelling patterns, unitized by phonology, begin to emerge as identifiable chunks (for example, rimes and affixes), further supporting sight learning.

Most significantly, the child now has strategies to read new words never before seen. These strategies enable the child to translate the printed word into a pronunciation. The child recognizes the word from the pronunciation, and the spelling quite readily becomes bonded to the spoken word.

Full alphabetic reading is supported not just by teaching the separate phonic letter values and applying them systematically to spellings, but by encouraging children to look at the words for spelling patterns which symbolize the constituent sounds.

STAGE 4: THE CONSOLIDATED ALPHABETIC PHASE

The consolidated alphabetic phase develops spontaneously from the 'chunking' processes of full alphabetic reading. Particular spelling sequences are now recognized within different words, so common spelling chunks come to be recognized as units. Such units may be onsets or final blends ('spr-', '-nk'), vowel digraphs ('-ee-'), rimes ('-est', '-ight'), syllables ('-tain'), prefixes ('con-', 'super-'), suffixes ('-ation', '-ly'), inflections ('-ed', '-ing'), or stems ('beauti-').

While these units are pronunciation units, many of them are, at the same time, morphemes (units carrying elements of meaning). Some pronunciation units, such as consonant blends and vowel digraphs (for example, 'gr-', '-oa-'), don't, in themselves, carry any meaning, but syllables may, and affixes, including inflections, invariably do. Thus, '-est' in 'rest' is not a morpheme, because it carries no meaning, but '-est' in 'prettiest' is. Recognizing such chunks as sub-word units is what the National Curriculum means by 'graphic knowledge'.

In the consolidated alphabetic stage, the brain learns to process spellings in terms of pronounceable chunks. These chunks become usable units through familiarity and reinforcement. Both meaning and pronounceability help to make the chunks memorable. A child at this stage who's never encountered 'entry' may say /en-try/, but only because she has 'chunked' the word into known, meaningful and pronounceable units.

Of course, most words encountered, being relatively short and frequent, are read as a single chunk. These are fully processed sight-words. The processing not only identifies all the letters and the order in which they occur but, because of the frequency with which the letters occur together, they mutually reinforce each other's identification. Such words are identified as swiftly as single letters.

Alongside the development of ever more subtle orthographic decoding goes a development in accessing meaning. Not only are pronunciations accessed directly from the spellings, but so are meanings. At the earlier stages of partial and full alphabetic reading, meaning tends to be accessed through pronunciation. The child sounds out the word and listens to hear if it is a known word. This way of accessing meaning means that the child cannot readily distinguish between homophones. For example, most children at six to seven years old will say that, 'Tell me wear he went' makes sense. But most children at ten will say it is nonsense (Harris and Coltheart, 1986). This is because, by this age, most children can access meaning directly from the spelling and not just from pronunciation.

TWO ROUTES TO WORD IDENTIFICATION

As adults we have two routes available for word identification: the phonological route, via pronunciation; and the orthographic route, directly from spelling. While meaning can be accessed without recourse to pronunciation, we never discard the phonological processes. We use them to tackle new words and as a back-up system for sight-word recognition.

There is evidence that, as adults, we habitually use both routes in parallel. We read familiar regular words (for example, horse, dance, quick) more quickly than we read either familiar irregular words (for example, laugh, come, build) or regular invented non-words (for example, gupont, wipasult) (Stuart, 1995). Irregular words are read by the orthographic route and non-words by the phonological route. But familiar regular words can be read both ways and, on average, the two routes working in parallel will be quicker than either route on its own.

The phonological route can operate at two levels. One level is deliberate and conscious, the other is not. At the unconscious level, this route, like the orthographic, operates automatically in the adult reader. So different is this from the laborious processes of sounding out that Stuart (1995) argues that there is 'no necessary relation the one to the other' (page 46).

This argument, however, ignores the point that automated, unconscious and complex skills are generally the product of over-learning skills that have initially been learned deliberately, laboriously and piecemeal. For dealing with new words, deliberate graphophonic translation remains an available strategy for occasional use. But the skills of reconstructing internalized pronunciations from spelling chunks, originally developed from deliberate graphophonic processes, continue to be employed pervasively at an unconscious level on complex and less frequent words.

CONCLUSION

Reading is not a simple, linear process but a complex, interactive web of skills. The main points to remember are that:

✧ reading as a self-correcting, self-tutoring process, can only develop based upon secure alphabetic skills;

✧ alphabetic skills include both visual identification and phonological skills, ie, graphophonic skills;

✧ the function of graphophonic skills is to establish flexible ways of mapping sounds onto spellings;

✧ building up an orthographic sight vocabulary depends upon the graphophonic processing of the sequence of letters in words as spelling-cum-pronunciation recognition units;

✧ skilled reading depends upon the orthographic sight recognition of virtually all words encountered, paralleled and supported by graphophonic processes.

The primary implication for teaching children to learn to read is that developing graphophonic/phonological skills is the key to overall development. Skilled readers possess a large sight vocabulary, initially developed through alphabetic skills learned in the primary years. This development is grounded in the processes of mapping sounds onto spellings. Initially, in the pre-alphabetic phase, links between the visual recognition of words and the phonological processes are non-existent. Teaching the alphabet begins to refine the visual perception of words and provide phonological help with their identification. Pronounceability and meaning help to organize the mapping of spelling patterns as recognition units.

The task of teaching reading, then, is largely a matter of developing phonological and alphabetic skills and teaching their use in the graphophonic translation of print into pronunciations, and in chunking spelling patterns as recognition units. At the same time, the teacher is concerned that children derive meaning from their reading and learn to use their expectation that texts should make sense to monitor their decoding skills. It is to the detail of this task that the rest of this book is devoted.

CHAPTER 2

DEVELOPING PHONOLOGICAL AWARENESS

'PHONOLOGICAL AWARENESS' AND READING

'Phonological awareness' is one of the key skills identified by the National Curriculum for reading at Key Stage 1: 'Pupils should... be made aware of the sounds of spoken language in order to develop phonological awareness.'

The National Literacy Strategy *Framework for Teaching* likewise emphasizes the basic importance of phonological awareness and says that children 'should be taught to discriminate between the separate sounds in words'.

Phonological awareness does not refer simply to the ability to recognize the words that you hear. Rather, it is an alertness to the constituent sounds *within* the words and the ability to *play* with those sounds. It is shown, for example, in the ability to recognize when one word rhymes with another and in the ability to find or invent further rhyming words. This is an ability that develops spontaneously: according to Chukovsky (1963),

> Rhyme-making during the second year of life is an inescapable stage of our linguistic development. Children who do not perform such linguistic exercises are abnormal or ill. (page 48)

It may not be immediately obvious why the ability to detect and produce rhymes should be so important – it seems odd that not attending to the *meanings* of words but, rather, attending to their *sounds* (which are merely the vehicle of meaning) should be important for developing reading. Yet research has clearly established that among pre-school children:

> ...phonological awareness proves to be a better predictor of reading development than performance on intelligence tests.
>
> (Ellis (1993), page 77)

There is also strong research evidence to show that struggling readers at Key Stage 2 typically have poor phonological skills, including being poor at identifying and producing rhymes. There is also evidence, though not so strong, that training in phonological awareness assists reading success (Bryant and Bradley, 1985; and Hatcher, Hulme and Ellis, 1995).

However, training in phonological awareness that relates *simultaneously* to the way sounds are represented in print (for example, showing how, by changing a letter, you can turn 'ham' into 'jam' and how the rhyming part stays the same) has been shown to have a very powerful effect on reading development with both normal and slower learners. The effects are both marked (with children's reading ages developing at up to twice the chronological rate) and long-lasting.

Hatcher, *et al* (1995) call the theory behind this the 'phonological linkage hypothesis'. It maintains that phonological skills and reading need to be explicitly linked to be effective. This is because phonological skills, by enabling children to identify the component sounds of words, help them to map the spoken words they know onto the written spellings they are learning. Phonological awareness is a precondition for this mapping to become possible.

Phonological awareness comes into existence spontaneously – for example, Slobin (1978) cites his three-year-old daughter playing, unprompted, with word sounds: 'Eggs are deggs. Enough duff. More bore'. And this awareness can be developed by parents and teachers prior to the child encountering print and the alphabet. Learning the alphabet will then help phonological awareness develop finer discriminations, for example, awareness of 'phonemes', the smallest units of sound used to distinguish between different words (for example, /heat/ and /hot/, /not/ and /what/) and which are largely represented in writing by individual letters or digraphs. Awareness of phonemes is a large part of what the *Framework for Teaching* (mentioned earlier) means by 'the separate sounds in words'. This more finely tuned awareness, in turn, helps with the development of flexible alphabetic reading skills. This chapter will, therefore, discuss phonological awareness both before and during the development of alphabetic knowledge.

THE PHONOLOGICAL SKILLS

Rhyming and alliteration are not the only phonological skills relevant to reading, though they appear early and are generally indicative of other skills. Other relevant phonological skills include:

✧ word repetition – the ability to hear a new word and repeat it correctly (not to be confused with the ability to say what the sounds are);

✧ hearing words as units – the ability to distinguish word boundaries in listening to speech;

✧ hearing syllables – the ability to distinguish the syllables in a word (to clap in rhythm to them, to articulate the pronunciation of a word according to the syllables, for example, /pump-kin/, /con-sta-ble/);

✧ discriminating onsets and rimes – the ability to recognize and produce alliteration and rhymes, and to segment syllables into onsets and rimes (for example, /c-at/, /spr-ing/);

✧ segmenting and ordering phonemes – the ability to analyse spoken words into their constituent phonemes and to recognize and remember their sequence (for example, /c-a-tch/, /s-p-r-i-ng/);

✧ blending phonemes – the ability to hold a sequence of phonemes in memory and pronounce them fluently together (for example, /h-a-v/→/have/, /or-t-uh-m/→/autumn/);

✧ naming – the ability instantly to identify and put a name to letters and words, for example, to identify A and a, G and g, as the same letter as quickly as being able to identify C and c.

✧ short-term auditory memory – the ability to recall word strings over a few seconds and rehearse them, for example, a telephone number or the wording of a phrase or sentence (essential for enabling sentences to be processed as complete units in the working memory);

✧ intonation patterns in phrases and sentences – the ability to produce the intonations patterns appropriate to the grammar and meaning of a sentence in fluent reading.

The significance of each of these skills will, I hope, become clearer as the argument of this book progresses. For the moment, it is important only to see that they constitute a broad range of skills involving auditory discrimination and memory, and that they operate across the twilight zone between the purely intuitive and the fully deliberate and conscious.

THE SOUNDS OF WORDS AND THE SOUNDS WITHIN WORDS

Words are made of sounds. And written words are made of symbols representing sounds. The child comes to reading equipped with her knowledge of spoken language, which includes knowing the sounds of many words. These include most of the words she is likely to encounter in early reading texts. But what does it mean, 'to know the sounds of words'? Even the way we talk about sounds and words can be confusing – we talk about the sound of a word and the sounds constituting a word. In the first case, we treat the sound of the word as a single unit, and in the second we treat it as consisting of smaller units, the smallest being phonemes.

In order to understand speech, we need to recognize words instantly in a unitary way. But before we can learn the analytic alphabetic skills of matching written spellings with the sounds of words we know, we need to become alert to the component sounds within the word. So, before we can match the letters of the word 'cat' with the sound-word /cat/, we need to be know that /cat/ consists of the sounds /c/ + /a/ + /t/.

The significance of the term 'phonological awareness' in the National Curriculum and The National Literacy Strategy *Framework for Teaching* is that it is drawing attention, above and beyond what is needed for speech, to the new kind of awareness of word sounds that reading demands. Before children learn to read or are encouraged to become reflective about spoken language, they may hardly be aware that individual words exist out of the streamy flow of sounds and meanings in speech. And they are not aware in any reflective way about the patterns of separate sounds within words.

Children learn new words as they hear and attend to them – from about the age of two-and-a-half they are very curious about language ('What is that?') and learn new vocabulary at a tremendous rate. But they don't always get the pronunciation or the boundaries right. Thus Jessica, at two, said /boh/ for 'boat', and at four, says /weat/ for 'eat' – presumably because it is difficult to hear where the word boundary occurs in the common phrases, 'What would you like to eat?', 'Will you eat it up, please?'

Being read to, seeing the discrete words of the text and learning that there is a one-to-one correspondence between the written word and its pronunciation, is often a key factor in establishing words as discrete perceptual units. It behoves the teacher to be alert to problems children might have with hearing word boundaries. Slow-learner David (Year 5) wrote 'onisolides' (for 'on his holidays') – and one cannot help but speculate about how far his apparent lack of auditory discrimination has contributed to his problems with literacy.

Word repetition games can usefully focus children's attention on word sounds as well as giving you, as a teacher, diagnostic information about children's auditory discrimination. It can even be fun to use nonsense words (glimp, grutch, spogue, nist, and so on). Children enjoy nonsense and can even invent their own, and they certainly don't depend on previous knowledge to identify the component sounds. You could include 'Nonsense News' at news time – 'Please, Miss, I saw a gluck on my way to school today. It was sproating an old fust.'

Sentence repetition and list repetition ('When I went shopping, I bought...') or cumulative repetition games like 'The Parson's Cat' ('The parson's cat is an awful cat. The Parson's cat is an awful, ugly cat...') involve different skills, skills to do with the short-term auditory memory. When reading begins, decoded words, read one at a time, need to be assembled to become grammatically coherent and make coherent sense. It is in the short-term memory that the words assemble into meaningful sentences.

What about the sounds within words? An early sign of growing awareness and reflectiveness about the sound patterns within words occurs spontaneously in children's alertness to, and enjoyment of rhyme. Rhyme is generally emphasized by rhythm, the rhythmic patterns of poems and nursery rhymes. Rhyme acts as an auditory end-marker for the lines as rhythmic units in poems, and these rhythms give rise to the expectation of a coming rhyme. But simple proximity can also highlight repetition of rhyming sounds – as in the names 'Humpty-Dumpty', 'Henny-Penny' and 'Goosey-Lucy'. Proximity and rhythm also highlight alliteration as in the phrases 'Jack and Jill', 'Baa-Baa Black Sheep' and 'Kitty Fisher found it'.

It is important here to distinguish between skills children use intuitively in practice and skills they are aware of and can reflect upon. Phonological awareness and reflectiveness are important for developing reading. Children are spontaneously alert to syllables – they can readily clap in time to the syllables in spoken language; and they can easily learn to segment words into their constituent syllables in a way that enables them to become reflectively aware of them. Similarly, they can learn to segment syllables into their constituent onsets and rimes (the parts that can alliterate and the parts that can rhyme).

But things are different at the phonemic level. Phonemes, as we said, are the smallest units of sound that are used to distinguish one word from another. While children can intuitively respond to these distinctions, they are not spontaneously aware of them. For many children, it is only learning the alphabet that prompts them into phonemic awareness. Yet flexible attentiveness and awareness of phonemes is vital for developing alphabetic reading skills.

PHONOLOGICAL PROBLEMS

There are some children for whom phonological skills, spontaneous or taught, present considerable difficulties. These children are at risk of finding reading problematic because, without a sense of the sounds in words, they will find mapping sounds onto spellings confusing. Such children can be identified early because they show difficulties with word repetition tasks, as well as rhyme and alliteration recognition.

Of course, all children have some problems with word repetition – Jessica, at three, called spaghetti 'basgetti' and could not be taught otherwise. She either did not hear or could not reproduce the (subtle) distinction between /p/ and /b/ and she 'unpacked' the 'sp-' consonant blend, separating the blended phonemes with a vowel and transposing them. It was easier to cope with two consonants across the syllabic divide ('-sg-') than within a blended syllabic onset. But at four she could spontaneously say 'spaghetti' (though still occasionally reverting to the earlier version).

However, Harry, aged eight-and-a-half and with severe reading problems, is cited by Goulandris and Snowling (1995) as calling spaghetti 'sagetti', then 'pasgetti' during a word repetition task. If he does not hear /sp-/ as /s/ + /p/, the spelling 'sp-' is not going to map consistently and meaningfully with anything in his knowledge of spoken language.

The Key Stage 1 teacher needs to be alert to unusually slow development in correct pronunciation. But, although the teacher needs to be attentive, not all errors are going to be long-term problems.

PLAYING WITH THE UNITS OF PHONOLOGY

What we are most likely to mean by phonological awareness is the ability to identify and play with the constituent sounds within words. Alertness to syllables, to rhyme and alliteration, and the constituent phonemes within words are the key requirements.

SYLLABLES

Each syllable in a word is centred on a vowel sound, which is a pulse of vocal energy. Thus the word 'syllable' has three such pulses – /syll-a-ble/ – and the word 'pulse' has one. Not every syllabic pulse, however, has the same energy. Some syllables are stressed compared with others and it is the pattern of stresses that give rise to rhythm. Rhythms are emphasized in poetry and nursery rhymes and most children will respond spontaneously to these rhythms. For example, group recitation of a nursery rhyme tends to turn, unprompted, into a highly rhythmic chant. Most children are readily able to beat time or clap in rhythm.

Similarly, children in general will be able to clap or beat time to the syllabic pulses of energy. That is to say, they will clap three times for 'Hickory dickory dock', or three times for 'hick-or-y', depending on which you draw their attention to and what pattern of clapping you model. While it could be easy for children to become confused between these two clapping patterns, demonstration and drawing explicit attention to the distinction between syllables and beat should make things clear.

ONSET AND RIME

Syllables are not the smallest units to which children are alert. Syllables can be sub-divided into the units of 'onset' and 'rime', thus:

ONSET	RIME
–	in
b	in
bl	inks

Rime is the part that might rhyme – that is to say, it is the vowel sound and anything that follows. The onset is anything that comes before the vowel sound. Children's alertness to rhyme indicates their alertness to rime as a unit. Alliteration doesn't correspond to onset in quite the same way. Alliteration may involve just the first letter sound or an initial consonant blend, for example:

> The bare, black cliffs clanged round him...
>
> (Tennyson)

The words 'bare' and 'black' only alliterate on the first consonant, but 'cliffs' and 'clanged' alliterate on the consonant blend that is the whole onset. Children cannot easily unpack the different consonant sounds merged in a blend, but they seem to respond to both patterns of alliteration. Rhyme tends to be more salient, however.

PHONEMES

Pre-reading children are generally alert to the phonological units mentioned so far.

But phonemic awareness does not seem to develop out of spoken language experience, but rather seems to develop as a result of teaching, and the introduction to alphabetic ways of looking at print. Thus, while children will be able to tell you how /bun/ and /pun/ are distinguished by their initial phonemes, because they are, at the same time, onsets, they will not be able so readily to identify the phonemic distinctions between /bun/ and /but/ or /bun/ and /bin/. Yet phonemic awareness is a critical skill for reading and writing.

Segmenting phonemes (separating out the constituent phonemes within words) does not come easily to children. And separating out the phonemes in a consonant blend, for example, /spr-/, is particularly hard. Goswami and Bryant (1990) call segmentation the 'phonemic hurdle' that children have to be helped to surmount. This help most generally takes the form of being taught letter/sound correspondences and applying them to words. But it is also possible to teach phoneme segmentation by purely phonological means, by playing phoneme counting, oral blending and segmentation games, discussed below.

PHONOLOGICAL AWARENESS TRAINING

Both rhyme detection, which comes earlier, and phonemic

awareness predict later reading success. For pre-readers, pre-alphabetic readers and early alphabetic readers, training in these areas has a beneficial effect (and an even greater beneficial effect when combined with visual exploration of words at the same time – see Chapters 3 and 5).

The following practical activities are intended to focus specifically on phonological awareness. They provide both training and opportunities for individual assessment.

PRE-SCHOOL AND PRE-READING ACTIVITIES

RHYME AND ALLITERATION

✧ Tell and teach nursery rhymes. Discuss the rhyming words – what makes them rhyme? Ask the children what other words rhyme with them.

✧ Play rhyme games. Ask the children to find rhymes for a given word or invent rhyming phrases ('Silly Billy', 'Messy Jessie', 'Sam likes jam') using the children's names. Encourage the children to anticipate the rhyme by leaving a suspenseful gap in your reading of a poem at the line ending. Play 'I spy...' or 'I hear with my little ear, something that rhymes with...'

✧ Play alliteration games. For example, 'Sam likes sandwiches', 'Emma likes eggs'; 'One wet wellie, two torn tambourines...'

✧ Play onset and vowel 'I spy'. 'I spy, with my little eye, something that begins with 'tay'. (For 'table'. This avoids the problem of saying /tuh/ for 'table' which is not pronounced /tuh-able/.)

✧ Play onset 'I spy'. 'I spy, with my little eye, something that begins with 'st'. (For 'stamp'. This doesn't avoid the problem mentioned above.)

✧ Invent picture rhymes. For example, show a clue picture (for example, a tie) and ask the children to choose a 'rhyming' picture from three pictures (for example, a book, a shirt, an eye).

SHORT-TERM AUDITORY MEMORY ACTIVITIES

✧ Continue repetition activities. 'One wet wellie, two torn tambourines...' (extend the list, as with 'The Parson's Cat'). Make shopping lists. Give a child a verbal list of items and ask her to repeat them. The other children can check whether she gets them right! Try message repetition. Give a child a verbal message to repeat, as in 'Chinese Whispers'.

✧ Play 'First and Last'. List four or five items and ask a child to name the first, the last, and so on. (The child has to rehearse the list in her head.)

RHYTHM AND SYLLABLES

✧ Experiment with rhythm. Ask the children to clap or tap to the rhythm (beat) of some nursery rhymes.

✧ Explore syllables. Try 'Sill-y Speak-ing' – speak-ing slow-ly to em-phas-ize the syll-a-bles (you might have a Space Teddy who can only understand such speech!). Note that 'Silly Speaking' can be extended for use in onset-rime segmentation, for example, 'M-y n-ame is S-am'. And this can be further extended to phoneme segmentation, for example, 'M-y n-a-me i-s S-a-m'.

✧ Ask the children to clap or count with counters to the syllables in spoken words.

PHONEME DISCRIMINATION

✧ Play 'Silly Speaking' as above.

✧ Play games to develop sound segmentation skills. For example, 'First sound I spy' with prolonged consonants – 'm', 'n', 'l', 's', 'f', 'v' (the consonants that can be pronounced without adding an /uh/ vowel sound, as in /cuh/).

✧ Now play traditional 'I spy'.

✧ Play 'The Magic Bridge'. To cross the bridge safely, the child must use the password formula, for example, 'My name is Dan. D-d-d-dan. D-d-d-d,' or 'I am a snake. S-s-s-snake. S-s-s-s'. Later, change the formula: 'I am a snake-k-k-k!', and so on.

✧ Categorize objects according to their initial sounds, for

instance, make collections for an /m/ table. Sort objects according to their initial sounds.

✧ Try 'sound dominoes', using picture cards. The last phoneme of one word links with the first phoneme of the next, for example, a dog – a goat – a tank – a cat, and so on.

✧ Play 'sound chains', like 'sound dominoes' above, but played orally, with children choosing any word that links.

✧ Try a variety of oral 'Odd Ones Out' (sound categorization) with lists of three or, later, four words. Try initial sound (alliteration) – 'pig, pet, hen, pie'; then try rhyme – 'hen, ten, sit, pen'; then try the last sound – 'sat, hip, top, pup'; and finally try assonance (vowel sound, which is quite hard) – 'hot, Tom, pig, lock'.

✧ Spot phonemes in words: 'Is there a /t/ in "Tom"?', 'Is there a /t/ in "hat"?', 'What sound can you hear at the end of "front"?'

PHONOLOGICAL ACTIVITIES FOR THE EARLY READING STAGE

✧ Introduce phoneme blending – 'What word do you get if you blend these sounds together /m/, /a/, /ch/?' (This is oral phonics!)

✧ Try phoneme segmentation. This is not easy for the children but the advantages of this activity outweigh the problems. 'Say the word 'mat' slowly. What are the sounds in it? Say them slowly, one at a time– /m/-/a/-/t/.' (Start with single consonant onsets and final consonants. Then move on to onset and final blends, for example, 'friend'.)

✧ Play with phoneme counting. Draw a row of boxes, with one box for each phoneme in the chosen word, for example, 'pig' (3). Say the word slowly and ask the child to put one counter in a box for each sound (phoneme) heard. Then ask the child to say the word s-l-ow-l-y, and you put a counter in a box for each sound heard. Finally, ask the child both to pronounce the word and put out the counters. (Developments of this task are discussed at greater length in Chapter 5.)

✧ Try splitting and blending oral activities. Ask the children, for example, to say aloud the first sound in 'hill' or 'pink'. Then ask them to leave out the first sound, for example, 'cake' becomes 'ache' and 'mice' become 'ice'. Now ask the children to put a /p/ onto the beginning of 'ink' and say the word aloud. What do they get? Then extend this by asking, 'What do you get if you put a /k/ at the end of "pin"?', 'What do you get if you leave the /k/ off "pink"?', 'What do you get if you leave the /s/ out of "nest"?', 'What do you get if you put a /k/ in the middle of "money"?', ' Can you take the /i/ from "pin" and put in /e/?'

✧ Using sounds in onsets and rimes. Ask the children to segment rimes into component phonemes, for example, 'friend' gives /e/-/n/-/d/. Then ask them to segment the blended onsets, for example, 'sc-', 'scr-', 'tr-', 'str-', etc.

Many of these activities can be developed using movable letters, so reinforcing notions of letter/sound correspondences.

CONCLUSION

A pre-school child's phonological awareness predicts later reading success and there is evidence that training increases phonological awareness. Phonological awareness is important because reading involves mapping sounds onto print and the child who is not alert to the constituent sounds within words will not find this mapping makes much sense. The National Curriculum says she should be given opportunities for 'recognizing alliteration, sound patterns and rhyme, and relating these to patterns in letters'.

If the child cannot recognize the sound patterns, she is in no position to relate them to spelling patterns.

The development of spelling/sound correspondences is facilitated by an alertness to the sounds. However, phonological training that, at the same time, maps sounds to the patterns of letters in words is even more successful. And so, we turn next to letters.

CHAPTER 3

TEACHING THE ALPHABET

Written words are made out of letters, and the sequence of the letters encodes the word's pronunciation. No wonder 'learning your letters' is virtually synonymous with 'learning to read'! But of course, the letters themselves have to be distinguished and the code understood before they can be used to identify words.

Children come to school with vastly different experiences of print. Even if they haven't yet learned their letters, some will have been read to a lot and will know that print is a special kind of visual information because it symbolizes spoken language. Some will have begun to understand how the system works, while yet other children, because print has no significance for them in their experience, may effectively not even see it all around them.

Print and word awareness need to be encouraged with pre-readers – and so does letter awareness. As discussed in Chapter 1, many children come to school recognizing certain words from environmental print, for example, shop names, logos and street signs. Much of this pre-alphabetic 'reading' depends on recognizing distinctive letter features. But this is not the same as 'knowing their letters'. One study deliberately replaced letters in logos to see if children could identify what was wrong; for example, in the Pepsi logo the name was spelled 'Xepsi'. As long as the logo retained its colour and shape, few pre-readers realized anything was wrong. This suggests that, with regard to discriminating letters, learning from environmental print is of limited value. Other features of the design were more visually salient than the letters 'P' and 'X'. And the differences between the letters 'C' and 'G' are even more elusive *if attention has never been explicitly drawn to letter shapes*. After all, as Adams (1990) says:

> In what reasonable kind of world would people agree to call both a dachshund and a St Bernard 'dogs' while calling one of these characters a 'C' and the other a 'G'? (page 345)

Exposure to letters is not enough. The teacher needs to teach children to attend to letters and their differences. One obvious way is through the child's own name. Not only does she learn to recognize it on the label for her peg and drawer, she learns to write it. And in learning to write it, the shapes and sequence of the letters are learned. The child can be encouraged to notice where her name letters occur elsewhere and, in doing so, learn the general points that words are made of letters and different letters are distinct from each other.

TEACHING THE ALPHABET

Teaching the alphabet – seems straightforward enough, doesn't it? But how do you teach it – one letter per week for 26 weeks? What do you teach – ay, bee, cee or /a/, /buh/, /cuh/? The letter names or the letter sounds? Do you teach the lower case letters first, a, b, c, or the upper case (capitals), A, B, C? Or do you teach them together? In what order do you teach the letters?

For reasons that I hope to explain, I shall tackle the process of teaching the alphabet in the following order:

- the sounds of the letter names;
- naming the letter shapes;
- exploring the letter shapes;
- letter sounds.

But let's start by considering the nature of the alphabet and what it does.

THE ALPHABETIC PRINCIPLE

Our written language operates on the alphabetic principle: that is, the letters, individually and in combinations, represent the language sounds. Spelling, in the first instance, is a code for writing the *sounds* of words, not their meanings. That's why you can read 'gluff' perfectly easily, even though it doesn't mean anything. A skilled reader can instantly decode the spelling into a pronunciation. This principle is not obvious to children, however. Byrne (1998) says:

> Children will not, for the most part, make the discovery unaided, and the consequences... of not discovering the alphabetic principle are serious. It follows that instructional methods that assume that the alphabetic principle need not be a prime, early focus... are ill-founded. (page 1)

However, the alphabetic principle is confused in English. One major reason is that there are only 26 letters but 44 sounds (phonemes) in English. So it is not simply a matter of learning one-to-one correspondences between letters and sounds as it is, for example, in Hindi. As a consequence, English has well over 350 spelling rules and is still notoriously irregular. Nevertheless, spelling is always a guide to pronunciation, even if one has to learn a spelling as a one-off, like 'yacht' (spelled 'yott' before Caxton's Dutch printers got hold of it!). Spelling irregularities often draw attention to themselves in ways that help us to remember them: for example, '-ight' is a very distinctive pattern and a very reliable guide to pronunciation.

Another reason is that spellings do two jobs at the same time. They tell you about pronunciation *and* they provide information about word meanings. It is more helpful to *see* that 'know' and 'knowledge' are related than to be informed about their differing pronunciations. This is why Venezky (1995) says that English has a 'morpho-phonic script'. As we shall see in Chapter 8, reading by morphemic chunks will supersede reading by letters – but this skill has to be based on a firm alphabetic foundation.

Byrne (1998) concludes that understanding the alphabetic principle is an essential precondition for print to become self-pronouncing, and that if we want children to understand the alphabetic principle, we should tell them about it!

In the first instance, the alphabetic principle is best illustrated by consonants, which generally retain a single sound value, especially at the beginnings of words. Exceptional pronunciations like 'c' in 'city', 'g' in 'giant', 's' in 'sugar' and 'h' in 'hour', are best bypassed until the general alphabetic principle has been established. On the whole, consonants are more reliable guides to pronunciation than vowels which all represent at least two different sounds, the name sound and the more usual phonic sound, for example, 'i' in 'kite' and 'kit'.

TEACHING THE ALPHABET: NAMES OR SOUNDS FIRST?

For centuries children were taught that 'cee' – 'ay' – 'tee' spelled 'cat'. Only in the last century did anyone think of teaching letter *sounds* instead of *names* and say *cuh – a – tuh* spells 'cat'. This raises the question, even with reliable consonants: do you teach letter names or letter sounds first? You need to get one of them reasonably well-established before starting on the other, or you risk confusion.

Traditional phonics tends to start with letter sounds as the most obvious route to phonic word-building. With a carefully regulated vocabulary, as in 'Nan and Dan are in the van' the child can experience success exploiting a sounding out and blending formula (though even here, the words 'are' and 'the' raise problems). Yet despite the obvious advantages of having letter sounds immediately available for use, there are stronger arguments for starting with letter names.

Research (see Adams, 1990, and Bryant and Bradley, 1985) suggests that, with pre-readers, knowledge of letter names (more than sounds or anything else) predicts future reading success. Why should this be so? I am impressed by the following argument, persuasively presented by Adams among others. In order for the child to learn the relationship between letter and sound, the child first needs a clear mental representation of each. With regard to the *visual* identity of letters, establishing the visual image of a letter is facilitated by giving it a name (the 'Rumplestiltskin' principle that naming confers mastery!). The name pulls together all the varied experiences of the letter – capital, lower case, different typefaces, different contexts, colours, sizes, feel, graphic movement, pronunciation, and so on

– so that they cohere in a developing concept, unified in the name.

Of course, if you choose, you can use the sound image as the conceptual focus. You can call a 'c' a 'cuh', or even a 'curly cuh', if you like. But this doesn't lessen the problems. It just creates different problems. The phonic value of the letter is not reliable, like the name, since 'curly cuh' sometimes says /s/. The letter name is easily pronounceable on its own, but letter sounds often aren't – the letter 'c' usually comes out as /cuh/, not /k/, because you can't enunciate the phoneme easily without adding the /uh/ vowel sound.

On the other hand, the letter *name* virtually always includes the sound. The name itself can act as a mnemonic for the sound. To say that learning the letter names first is best is not to deny that learning letter sounds is essential. But the name may help the child get a secure grasp on the letter as a *visual* identity and later act as a secure hook for learning the sound.

ILLUSTRATED ALPHABETS AND PICTOGRAMS

Sound-only approaches tend to rely on key word pictures or pictograms to act as mnemonics. In the case of pictures, the child learns the sound value in a word context – an illustration of an apple is read as '/a/ is for "apple"', and so on. With such illustrations, it is important that the onset of the key word is a single consonant because this isolates the phoneme as a perceptual unit. Clever cats, brown bears, crocodiles, frogs, grasshoppers, and so on, with their initial blends, don't provide clean-cut, single phoneme onsets.

Illustrations do not help with the *visual* identification of letters. However, pictograms (for example, where the letter 'a' is made into an apple, as in HarperCollins' *Letterland*) are generally more successful. Ehri *et al* (1984) found that using pictograms integrating letters, key words and pictures resulted in better retention of letter/sound correspondences than simple side-by-side letter and picture presentations.

TEACHING THE SOUNDS OF THE NAMES OF THE LETTERS

Learning the letter names is best undertaken in two stages: first, learning the names; second, relating the names to the shapes. The first task is to establish familiarity with the names. The most child-friendly approach is through learning to sing the alphabet, just like a nursery rhyme. It is possible to sing it to the tune of 'Twinkle, twinkle, little star...', but I've never quite got the hang of it! There are two more syllables in the tune than letters in the alphabet. I feel more comfortable with the chant I learned as a child:

As far as the children are concerned, at first it is simply a nonsense rhyme or chant that they learn to sing.

THE NURSERY RHYME GAME

Singing the alphabet has its place in the nursery rhyme game. Divide the class into two teams. One team starts singing a nursery rhyme and at the end you all sing the alphabet together. When it's finished, the other team sings a different nursery rhyme and you all sing the alphabet again. No repetition is allowed! Carry on until one team has run out of nursery rhymes. The team that can think of most rhymes is the winner. Or you can all sing together, or with children singing the rhymes they think of individually. Continue till you or the nursery rhymes are exhausted!

TEACHING THE ALPHABET: UPPER OR LOWER CASE FIRST?

This question is not as easily answered as you might suppose. Adams (1990), like others before her and responding to the fact that most environmental print is in capitals, argues that, for pre-school children, it might be best to teach upper case first. Further, upper case letters are more visually distinct from each other than are lower case letters. Then, contrarily, she points out that, since texts in school are printed in lower case, it is best for children to be taught lower case first in school. Very confusing!

What is fairly clear, however, is that to teach upper and lower case together can be even more confusing to the child. It is generally best to keep confusables apart in teaching – to get one thing reasonably well-established before broaching the other. The same thing applies to teaching the confusing letters, such as, 'b' and 'd', 'p' and 'q'.

It is probably best to teach lower case first, but to explain to the children that there are such things as capitals – after all, they will have experience of using them at the beginning of their own names! If the alphabet frieze has both lower case and upper case on it, so much the better: it can be used for reference when coming across upper case in texts. Learning the upper case will tend to happen piecemeal and spontaneously for most of the children. This is facilitated by the fact that many of them are, in any case, versions of the lower case shape, for example, Cc, Ss. It is easy to point out how even 'M' and 'm' are alike.

TEACHING LETTER NAMES

If the children have learned the alphabet song, then they will appear to know the names of the letters when you introduce the alphabet frieze. Though, of course, they don't yet know the shapes that accompany the names. Probably the children will tend to gallop through the song, and getting them to pronounce all the letter names distinctly is not easy. But with the frieze as text, you can slow them down and show them how it corresponds to the names they know, thus refining their enunciation. While singing the song, you point to the letters. Alternatively, ask the children to point or ask the children individually to point or stand up when you reach his or her name's initial letter. At first, this is just a matter of establishing a one-to-one correspondence between letters and names. But as you draw attention to the distinctive shapes of the letters, they start to acquire their own distinctive characters.

USING THE CHILD'S OWN NAME FOR LETTER IDENTIFICATION

It is in terms of their own names and learning to write them that children can most readily be introduced to the names, sounds and shapes of letters as a unity – especially if supported by pictograms. Many children may well be able to write their names before they come to school and to tell you the initial letter of their names. In any event, they should learn them as soon as possible for naming and identifying pieces of work. Copy cards are appropriate aids.

Finding 'their own letters' on the alphabet frieze is a thrill. Names can be tied like balloons to the appropriate place on the frieze. Sorting through letters to find their own initial letter gives a sense of ownership. They can play 'Name-snap', turning up letter cards and children claiming their own initial letters – or, more ambitiously, claiming any letter in their own names so that it becomes a kind of 'Name-Bingo' (though there have to be enough letters to go round!). Insist they name the letters as part of the game.

LEARNING THE SHAPES OF THE LETTERS

Of course, knowing the names of the letters in the song and knowing the letters in the frieze is not the same as knowing and recognizing individual letters out of context. You need to establish the visual characters of the individual letters. For successful reading, easy visual familiarity with, and identification of, the letters is crucial. Children who are not secure in visual letter identification are at a permanent and cumulative disadvantage. Naming them is helpful in establishing this familiarity and it also seems to mediate the relationship between each letter's shape and its sound value. Naming also helps to establish the equivalence between upper case and lower case letters.

TALKING ABOUT LETTER SHAPES

Familiarity with shapes can be developed in a number of ways, both visually and in terms of the feel of the movements used to draw them. There are many kinds of activities and games, homemade and proprietary, that can help. But whatever activities you use, *discussing the letters' shapes* while doing so is invaluable in order to focus attention. Children need to have their attention drawn to which visual characteristics *are* significant for distinguishing between letters – and also to those differences that are *not* important. You need to introduce them to different typefaces, to establish that a letter is the same letter, whatever its size, thickness or colour. Eventually it is important for the children to know the upper case and lower case form of each letter. As touched on above, children can explore which letters are the same shape when upper and lower case, for example, C/c, O/o, W/w, and which are a little different, for example, Y/y, P/p, I/i and which are very different, for example, A/a, N/n, R/r. But even with these last letters the 'a's have a hole in them, the 'n's are like shorter 'm's, the 'r's curl over at the top.

Some commercially available materials – alphabet jigsaws, foam letters – don't seem to take account of issues like 'Which way up?' or 'Which way round?' Movable letters should indicate which way up they should lie, otherwise children might reverse and invert them – 'b', 'd', 'p' and 'q' all become interchangeable! But problems like these can, and should, lead to class discussion about the importance of orientation, which letters are like each other in what ways, the importance of ascenders and descenders in distinguishing '**a**' and '**d**', '**a**' and 'q', 'h' and 'n'. (By the way, children don't know that terms like 'ascenders' and 'descenders' are difficult! Giving them a language for discussion focuses perception, just as giving names to letters focuses perception on them.)

THE IMPORTANCE OF MULTI-SENSORY LEARNING

Learning about letters is one of the many areas in which reading and writing reinforce one other. Letter shapes need to be known not only visually but also at the fingertips. The right sequence of movements to draw the letter shapes correctly should be practised on a large scale as well as small, as in air-writing, pattern painting with letters and on the board. This helps to establish the kinaesthetic model of each letter. Saying the letter names at the same time as writing them helps confirm the learning. And feely letters, for example, velour, can be textured to encourage the right movements. Such multi-sensory approaches have a long and respectable history, from Montessori onwards – she used sandpaper letters, but what this did to her scissors, I don't like to think! Anyway, nowadays you can buy sandpaper letters.

When teaching children to write the letters, these are important points to bear in mind:

✧ discuss the shapes and the distinctive elements to establish a vocabulary with which the children are comfortable. Also discuss the sequence of writing the letter, for instance, 'Start at the top and come back and round in a swirly snake shape';

✧ tracing should be avoided. This can be done mindlessly, and you want the shaping and the naming to go through the child's mind to reinforce the learning;

✧ shapes should be formed correctly in the way the pencil moves around the letter. Following dotted shapes, with starting points and arrows, is helpful in the beginning. Guidelines to indicate height of ascenders, etc., remain useful for some time. (I hate 'a's that look like 'd's and vice versa!);

✧ copying tends to ensure the letter shape is visually

processed. But the teacher *must* keep a close eye on things to ensure bad habits don't creep in. Incorrect movement sequences around the letter shapes are very hard to unlearn;

✧ children should be encouraged to pronounce the letter names while writing them, and even to talk to themselves about the shapes while writing, for example, 'Ay. Start at the top and round we go, back up to the top and down.'

APPROACHES AND ACTIVITIES TO REINFORCE LETTER LEARNING

From the start, deliberately use and exploit the letters you have taught, asking children to point them out in words they meet or to name them in what you are writing. Iversen (1997) suggests starting with the 'heavy duty' letters (Ss, Mm, Bb, Hh, Tt, Rr, Ff, Cc, Ww, Pp and Ll) which are going to be the least confusing and most used. Concentrating on a few letters, she teaches upper and lower case together. As for the rest of the alphabet, she reckons that 'most children will be able to learn the rest incidentally'. This policy of depending on incidental learning, however, is not as appropriate to our graphophonic emphasis as it is to her more 'language experience' orientated approach.

There are innumerable commercial letter sorting and matching games, letter shaping worksheets, and so on, available, and there are games and materials you can make yourself. What you need to be clear about is what each activity is teaching or reinforcing, and how effectively it is doing it. Some possible games and activities include:

✧ letter hunts – the child highlights all letters that occur in his or her own name on a throwaway text (perhaps a page from a magazine). As a variation, the child highlights as many instances of a given letter as possible within a given time limit;

✧ the letter naming game – played a bit like 'Snap' but using letter names. Turn up the letter cards one at a time. The successful 'namer' keeps the card. Variations include giving each child in turn a first chance to answer; mixing upper and lower case letters and using different typefaces; or encourage the children to play on their own;

✧ naming the letters in a word – the teacher reads and holds up a word card so the whole class can see it. Each child is given a turn to name the letters, winning the card if successful. Variations include doubling the score if the child can read the word as well;

✧ ask the children to write letters in a word as you dictate them – score a point for each correct letter and double points if the child can read the word;

✧ equivalences between letters in different type faces – sort, using letters stuck on cards, and develop this into a letter hunt with the children cutting out various letter examples from magazines;

✧ equivalences between upper and lower case forms – upper and lower case letters packs are needed, to be played like 'Snap'. When all the letters are paired, they should be shuffled and sorted back into their two original packs;

✧ feely bag letters – put some plastic letters into a feely bag. The feeler picks a letter and identifies it by feel, then takes it out for others to check if the identification is correct.

TEACHING LETTER SOUNDS

Teaching the letter sounds comes later, but not too much later. Confidence in identifying the letters by name is a good basis for starting to learn their sounds. The children have something secure to relate to the sounds. You can keep the distinction clear by referring to letter *names* and letter *sounds*, to what a letter is *called* and to what a letter *says*.

For children who come to school knowing their letters, learning the sounds can begin straightaway. But for children who do not know the letters, to teach shapes and sounds at the same time is confusing, difficult and slow. As a teacher, if you try to teach them together, you don't know whether any problems that occur are to do with learning the sound or to do with identifying the letter, and neither does the child.

Use the letter names when teaching the sounds, pointing out that the name generally contains the sound – but don't do too many at once. You can group them according to your phonic scheme, for example, using the short vowel sounds and the commonest initial consonants (for example, s, m, b, h, t, r, f, c, w, p, l, d). Or you can start with the child's own name. Practise cumulatively, using a variety of activities, including using the frieze and pictograms, letter Snap, pairs, plastic letters in feely bags, flash cards, variations on 'I spy', using initial phonemes and letter names, and so on. Practise letter-to-sound and sound-to-letter, for example, by identifying things in a picture that start with a given letter and group objects by their initial letters.

USING PICTURE CARDS AND LETTERS

✧ Sort picture cards into initial (or final) letter categories according to sound.
✧ Play dominoes, with a picture and letter (not matching) on each card.

To a great extent, once letter shapes and names are secure, letters sounds are learned incidentally. By the time you get round to focusing on phonics, you will be reinforcing and securing learning that is already familiar.

CONCLUSION

In order to be able to read fluently, to learn phonics and to be able to perceive the letter strings of words as spelling patterns, children need first to be able to identify the individual letters instantly. Failure to be able to do so is crippling. In order to be able to identify the letters instantly, children need to construct clear concepts of the letters for themselves. Such concepts most readily crystallize around the name of the letter. The name, the shape and the sound are best learned in that order. The shape is learned by naming and shaping it, assisted by explicit discussion of discriminating features. Only when the name and shape are reasonably secure should the question of sound (phonemic value) be intensively tackled.

CHAPTER 4

TEACHING A FIRST SIGHT VOCABULARY

This chapter deals with teaching an initial, pre-alphabetic sight vocabulary to give Reception children an encouraging start to reading. In Chapter 1, we considered what we might mean by a 'sight vocabulary'. The relevant points discussed were as follows:

✧ ultimately, effective reading depends upon being able to identify the vast majority of words we encounter at sight;

✧ how we identify sight-words changes from the pre-alphabetic stage through to the consolidated stage;

✧ at the pre-alphabetic stage, words tend to be recognized in idiosyncratic ways from arbitrarily selected visual features;

✧ pre-alphabetic sight-words in general have to be taught; the child has, as yet, no system for working words out;

✧ such rote-learning works equally well for regular and irregularly spelled words.

LOOK-AND-SAY TEACHING

Whole-word sight learning tends to occur, to some extent, spontaneously prior to the child's coming to school. Some of this learning results from everyday child/adult dialogue where the adult points out significant words in the environment, such as signs, shop names and notices. And some of this learning results from the child's own inferences about the functions of print, for example, assuming that labels name the objects to which they are attached. Such inferences may be erroneous – for example, a child who infers that the name 'Crest' says 'toothpaste'!

Teachers tend to exploit children's ability to learn whole words in order to help them experience some initial success in their early reading. It can be argued that it is easier for a child to learn 26 distinctive and meaningful words than 26 similar looking and meaningless letters. Since 12 key words (including he, the, it, was) make up a quarter of all the printed words a child encounters (McNally and Murray, 1968) and 100 key words make up more than a half, learning these words as sight-words seems to make sense. Especially as a very high proportion of these words are irregular and would not lend themselves readily to phonic learning processes!

Although this argument underpins the list of sight recognition words in the National Literacy Strategy *Framework for Teaching*, the logic of the approach doesn't itself translate entirely successfully into practice. It is commonly argued (for example, Browne, 1996) that such rote-learning can place a considerable strain on young children's memories, and that the traditional method of teaching with flash cards is more likely to produce boredom and misunderstandings about the nature and purpose of reading than to create fluent and enthusiastic readers.

Beyond a certain limited selection of key words, there is little agreement between whole-word schemes about which words to teach – so learning one scheme equips the child only for that scheme and not for a wider array of books. The limited selection of key words that all schemes agree on tend to be function words like articles, conjunctions, pronouns and prepositions which don't, in themselves, mean very much outside a sentence (you can't pin down 'which' with a mental image as you can 'witch'), and are consequently not as memorable. Meaning tends to inhere much more in the content words (for example, nouns and verbs) which tend not to be encountered as frequently. And the key words are bound, simply because they *are* key words, to occur in *any* text, whether it is explicitly key-word orientated or not.

Nevertheless, while teaching key words is not a complete answer to the question of how to teach reading, the rote-learning of key words has a crucial role to play, whether it is tackled by direct teaching or whether they are picked up in the course of shared reading. The National Literacy Strategy *Framework for Teaching* lists 45 sight recognition words for Reception, another 150 or so for Years 1 and 2, and yet more for Years 3, 4 and 5. The National Literacy Strategy *Framework for Teaching*, like the National Curriculum, specifies this whole-word learning under the heading 'Word recognition'.

It is fairly typical in schools for children to be taught pre-alphabetic sight recognition for a couple of terms before any letter/sound correspondence (phonic) skills are introduced. Many reading schemes are based on exploiting whole-word rote-learning in the early stages, even if they are a little cautious of claiming a 'look and say' approach for example, Ginn's *New Reading 360*, Heinemann's *Storyworlds* and older schemes like *1,2,3 and Away*.

The teacher's task is to find a way to teach an initial sight vocabulary that exploits the child's propensity to sight learn words that are of interest, and to do it in such a way that the learning does not become a dull rote-learning exercise, but has the potential to absorb and integrate developing alphabetic knowledge into itself.

ENVIRONMENTAL PRINT

A first vocabulary is learned from two different sources: words encountered in context in daily life, such as 'BUS STOP' (environmental print); and words which are expressly taught in school. If parents draw attention to environmental print ('Look, it says 'PUSH' on the door. So let's push it.'), then children are at least going to learn to notice print and to learn something of its functions and importance in daily life. And perhaps the child will learn to recognize 'PUSH' when she sees it and, with help, learn to distinguish it from 'PULL'. Though whether she will recognize the words out of their context on a door is a different matter!

Some reading schemes, old and new, pay a good deal of attention to environmental print, for example, *Link-up* and *The Flying Boot*. Much has been made of environmental print, and teachers feel obliged to put up all sorts of notices and labels in the classroom to help create a relevant print-rich environment. Yet children hardly notice, and learn little from this sort of print around the classroom. Unless, that is, the teacher makes a point of expressly drawing attention to it. Further, as we have seen, if children are left to infer word identities from context for themselves, they may get them wrong.

Environmental print around the classroom needs to be explicitly used as a teaching resource if it is going to be worthwhile. For example, when a new label or notice is put up, for example, 'wet paintings here, please', the teacher might ask if the children can see any new notices in the classroom and ask them to suggest what it might be about, using the context as a clue. Then the teacher should ask them to look at the words as she tells them what it says, and ask the children to read them back as she points to the words one by one. The teacher should discuss the distinguishing features of the words and ask the children to relate them to any other words they know as a way to help them remember the words.

WHAT CUES DOES A CHILD USE?

How does a child recognize a sight-word? There remains some disagreement between researchers as to what exactly is happening in rote-learning a sight vocabulary at the pre-alphabetic phase. For example, at one time it was thought that children learned an outline word shape, but now this seems to be largely discounted. Seymour and Elder (1985) showed that children were very nearly as good at recognizing:

y l o
e l w

as they were at recognizing the word in its normal configuration. That is, letter features, rather than outline shape, appeared to be critical. Indeed one boy, knowing 'yellow', identified 'smaller' as saying 'yellow' because it had 'two sticks in the middle'. He was using distinctive letter details rather than the global configuration as a clue for word identification.

Beginning readers, then, only 'remember selected cues to read sight-words' (Ehri, 1995). That is, though recognized on a purely visual or 'pictorial' basis (to use Ellis', 1993, term), they are not learned as global configurations. The visual basis may be to do with recognizing context, the logo style, accidentals like colour schemes or the typeface (Toys 'Я'Us), individual letter features (the 'two sticks' in 'yellow'), or even part-letter features, like the boy who could read 'television' 'because of the dots'.

There is plenty of scope for children to misunderstand what the significant differentiating features are between words – just as there is between letters. And how could it be otherwise? Until they have been taught the letters, how are they to know that letters are the significant elements in words? On the whole, however, it now seems that the words of a first sight vocabulary are largely learned from picking on letter details by which to identify each word.

SPONTANEOUS INFERENTIAL LEARNING

In addition to identifying words from odd letters, Margaret Clark (1976) found there are some children who come to school having apparently taught themselves to read by working out letter/sound correspondences for themselves. Similarly, Ellis (1993) argues:

> there may never be a stage for (some) children at which word recognition is purely pictorial; these children may utilise some degree of phonic decoding from the outset.
>
> (page 86)

For some children, there may not necessarily be such a quantum leap from the pre-alphabetic stage to the partial alphabetic stage as might first appear.

Goswami and Bryant (1990) speculate that:

> a great deal of... development takes the form of children just getting gradually better at strategies which they use right from the start. (page 147)

The strategies to which they are referring are inference-making strategies, with the child trying to make sense of the relationship between spoken words and print. The child latches onto correspondences from the start, but these may not be the important correspondences. The child almost certainly needs help to focus on the significant correspondences – which are sound/spelling correspondences.

Whether children begin to work out these correspondences for themselves or need to have their attention directed towards them, there is a clear moral for the teacher. Since children spontaneously tend to pick on letter features in learning sight-words, and progress in reading depends upon developing alphabetic letter/sound correspondence strategies, it behoves the teacher, in teaching a sight vocabulary, to draw attention to the significant letter features in the words, and not leave it solely to the child to decide what arbitrary features to latch onto for recognition purposes. The teacher should try to engage and direct children's spontaneous inference-making abilities towards remembering and making sense of words. The aim, ultimately, is to establish the sight-word as a fully processed recognition unit. And this means analysing the word in terms of the sequence of letters composing it.

Working towards this goal requires specific assessment and teaching strategies on the teacher's part. Most immediately, it means teaching sight vocabulary words in such a way as to encourage the child to focus on the letter structure of the word. For example, with the child who read 'smaller' as 'yellow', you might start by writing the two words one above the other and discussing similarities and differences.

EXPLOIT LETTER KNOWLEDGE AS SOON AS POSSIBLE

In parallel with teaching sight-words, you will be teaching the alphabet. To integrate the children's learning, it makes sense to use whatever alphabetic knowledge the child possesses as soon as possible in your sight vocabulary teaching. After all, this is what children do spontaneously! Even before they know the whole alphabet, they will use alphabetic cues where they can. They will latch onto letters they feel at home with as significant features. You can exploit and direct these propensities to maximize their effect. Some children may come to school knowing their letters or, at least, the letters of their names. And from the beginning, you will be starting to teach them the alphabet. So, exploit whatever letter knowledge is available in teaching sight-words!

In drawing attention to distinctive letter features, it is sensible to alert children to the letters they know in words they are learning and, sometimes, to the sounds symbolized by them. It makes sense to look at 'look' and 'book' together and discuss how they both rhyme and look the same; or notice how 'Jack' and 'Jill' start with the same letter and the same sound. In doing this, it is not so much that you are embarking on a fully phonic approach to teaching, but that you are beginning to show the children how the things they are learning fit together; and, at the same time, you are alerting the children to the general principle of sound/spelling correspondences in print. Using whatever letter knowledge they have already acquired does two things: it focuses the children's attention on the significant (letter) features of words and it begins to give children a strategy for thinking about the relationship between these features and the sounds of the words.

Thus, while the main part of what you are doing is teaching sight-words, you are also helping that sight recognition to be more complete and more analytic. It does not matter that this is not teaching pure look-and-say or pure phonics. It is good pedagogy, modelling ways for the children to develop their own strategies for looking at words and to apply their own active intelligence to the task; relating what you are doing with reading, with the alphabet and with phonological skills; and proffering ways for the children to make inferences beyond those you are explicitly teaching. Hopefully, the way we do this, even if it involves flash cards, will provide mnemonic support for memorizing words and will not be as mindless and mechanical as unfocused rote-learning.

PRACTICAL CLASSROOM APPROACHES

Each reading scheme is designed around its own particular approach. Part of the aim of this book is to provide a basis for interpreting the advice given in the teacher's guides and for adapting and developing the approach in a more balanced way, if this is needed. In the nature of things, schemes that don't start with phonics must start with whole-word learning. Where they differ is in how they expect whole words to be learned – either by direct teaching through the use of flash cards or similar aids, or incidentally in the process of sharing books, as in language experience approaches. However, a more balanced approach will hopefully maintain the supportive and motivational features of language experience and shared reading approaches, but will, in addition, promote an attentiveness to the printed form of the word in a way that readily develops into alphabetic processing.

The immediate aim of establishing a first sight vocabulary is to enable the child to experience the success of reading a whole book independently as soon as possible. Consequently, the sight vocabulary you teach will start with the words and phrases of the first reading books.

One possible approach would be to teach all the words individually on flash cards before letting the child see the book, then, lo! when she is given the book, she will be able to read it! But such initial rote-learning might be a rather deadly, mechanical process, divorced as it would be from a meaningful story.

The alternative approach, adopted in 'language experience' reading schemes such as Nelson's *Story Chest* and Heinemann's *Storyworlds*, is to familiarize the child with the stories through shared reading so that the child effectively learns the story by heart and, alongside this, learns to recognize more and more of the words. This a piecemeal process, with the child, during repeated shared readings, joining in with the remembered or recognized bits. The stories contain a lot a repetition to encourage this process. The idea is that the child learns the words almost as a by-product of enjoying the story.

Storyworlds exploits the potential of shared reading particularly imaginatively in the early stages, where, on a double spread, the left-hand page is designed for the teacher to read and the right-hand for the children. The left-hand page advances the action and the right-hand page is a refrain with repeated wording, part of the patterning of the story. However, in all shared reading approaches the chances of the children learning the words *out of the context* of the story are slight, if they have not been encouraged to examine them as individual words.

Familiarity with the story provides support and motivation, but the words need to be looked at separately if they are to be recognized in different contexts. Let's start by sharing and enjoying the story and then looking at the words and learning them, so that they can be used by the child in re-reading.

TEACHING SIGHT-WORDS

Start with a sentence from the story written out on a strip of card. Then match this with the same sentence in the book. Explain that you are now going to cut the strip up into individual words – ask the children to tell you where to cut. Individual words can then be picked out for examination and discussion. Shuffle the word cards and use them as flash cards for checking recognition. The final step is to put the cards back together again as a sentence – this requires word recognition, matching and a sense of meaning. The children can check the sentence again, against the book, to confirm that it is right.

Many of the first words you want to establish in the children's sight vocabulary are the common function words or the basic key words – 'is', 'was', 'a', 'the', 'on', 'in', 'from', and so on. Since these words occur very frequently in reading they are both needed early and practised often. Yet, because they are function words, children often tend not to notice them; 'cat' means something, but 'the' on its own doesn't. So it can be useful sometimes to include function words on the flash cards.

TEACHING KEY FUNCTION WORDS

Imagine you are looking at the words in the sentence 'The dog chased my cat up the tree.' You may want to explain that 'the' and 'The' are equivalent and why, or you may choose, for the occasion, to start the sentence with the lower case version. You can prepare duplicate cards for 'tree', 'the tree' and 'up the tree'. The single word cards enable you to concentrate on the identifying features of the individual words. The phrase card gives you the opportunity to discuss the number of separate words on the card and the rhythm of saying the phrase. The preposition 'up' and the article 'the' make more sense in the context of the phrase. You can compare other cards with 'the' on them, for example, 'the tree' and 'the dog', as well as 'up the tree', in order to establish the common feature between them. Comparing 'up the tree' with phrases like 'round the tree' gives you a chance to highlight the significance of function words.

LOOKING AT WORDS

We want children to be able to discriminate between different words in their pre-alphabetic sight vocabularies. How are we to encourage children to look with discrimination at words and their component letters in a pre-alphabetic, pre-phonic way?

In looking at words individually, you will want to ask the children about the right way to look at a word (from left to right), about how many letters there are, if they know any of the letters in the word and about whether they recognize any of the letters, for instance, from their own names. Ask whether they know what the letters are called and what sound the letters make. If anyone knows the sound of a letter, work at getting them to hear the sound in the word. If not, simply move on to the next stage, looking at the letter shapes and the patterns they make. For example, you might look at the risers and descenders in 'dog' and how all the letters have a hole in the middle, how 'tree' ends with two letters the same. (In some circumstances you might be able to relate this pattern to a rhyming word.) Ask the children to air-write the letter shapes.

You might want to construct a copy of the word with plastic letters by asking the children to select or tell you which letters are needed and in what order. You can try to cheat them by including a wrong letter or putting them in the wrong order and encouraging them to tell you why it is wrong and what it should be. What you are doing is drawing the children's attention to the visual features that are going to be significant for reading, so that what they focus on for identification is going to have a future value for them.

After looking at the letter composition of certain words, you can return to the sentence you are examining with the children.

Check the recognition of the words individually, re-read the sentence to the children and riffle through the cards, asking them to identify the first word, then the second and so on, until you have re-formed the sentence. Then ask them to read the sentence over again for fluency and meaning. The word cards can be kept in an envelope with the sentence written on it for future reference and revision. This whole process places the rote-learning clearly within a context of meaning.

PARENTAL HELP

It can be helpful to provide word cards in a tin for children to take home to practise with their parents. But before doing so, two things are important. One is to look at and discuss the words with the children in a class or group session prior to their being sent home so that the homework is a revision of things done in class. The other is to engage the parents' sympathetic support and their understanding of the aim of the exercise. You don't simply want to transfer the dull routines of rote-learning to the parents!

What you can ask of them is a simplified version of what you have done in the classroom. You provide a copy of the sentence and the word cards, and ask the parents to read the sentence with their child. They encourage the child to match the words on the card with the words in the sentence, then to shuffle the cards and name each word. The children put the word in its rightful place under the sentence until the sentence is complete, and then read the sentence. What is crucial is that this should not become a stressful experience – it should be treated as a game and, if the child is reluctant to play, it should not be forced on the child. Any pattern of reluctance, however, should be reported to the teacher for exploration.

CONCLUSION

A good reader has a large sight vocabulary. But this vocabulary is as much a consequence as a cause of being a good reader. For the good reader, the sight vocabulary consists of fully analysed recognition units or mental word templates. An initial sight vocabulary, however, is largely unanalysed: a word is likely to be recognized from only partial cues. Nevertheless, this shaky grasp can be built upon by paying deliberate attention to the significant patterns of letters in their sequence. Learning an initial sight vocabulary has these positive points:

✧ it builds on spontaneous processes;

✧ it quickly provides some initial experience of success;

✧ it enables the child to read frequently encountered words, including those with irregular spellings;

✧ the processes of recognition can be edged towards more alphabetic processes.

The negative points are that:

✧ mere rote-learning can be boring;

✧ rote-learning can lead to the idea that reading is simply about recognition and not about meaning;

✧ unanalytic, partial cue recognition processes cannot always differentiate between different words, and this limits the vocabulary and its usefulness.

However, these negative points can be countered by teaching approaches that ensure learning has pay-off in meaning and that ensure that the recognition strategies become more discriminating as they are developed towards more alphabetic and analytic processes.

CHAPTER 5

BEGINNING GRAPHOPHONICS

LINKING PHONOLOGICAL AND ALPHABETIC SKILLS

The term 'graphophonics' covers the whole range of ways in which the sounds and the written system of the language are related. The term links the alphabetic concept of 'graphemes' (the written equivalents of phonemes) with 'phonics' (the relation between graphemes and spellings on the one hand, and the phonological or sound system of the language on the other). Graphophonics, therefore, covers the mapping of sounds onto spellings, phonics and much of what is meant by 'phonological skills' when related to reading, as well as the skills of translating written language into pronunciations. This chapter is concerned with starting to make the links between phonological and alphabetic skills. It begins with a discussion of the crucial importance of these links and then picks up on how these links can be begun as soon as alphabetic knowledge starts to become available in the task of identifying words. Part Three continues the themes begun here.

THE 'PHONOLOGICAL LINKAGE HYPOTHESIS'

In Chapter 2, we touched on Hatcher *et al*'s (1995) 'phonological linkage hypothesis' which suggested that reading develops best where phonological skills and alphabetic skills are explicitly linked in teaching. Sound/spelling correspondences come to be exploited most successfully as a reading strategy where children have both clear perceptions of the sounds within words and are clearly shown how certain sounds regularly correspond with certain letters and letter strings.

The rationale behind the hypothesis has been around since at least 1985, but it was only given the name 'phonological linkage' by Peter Hatcher and his colleagues in relation to a study undertaken in Cumbria (P. Hatcher, C. Hulme and A. W. Ellis, 1995). They built upon the work of Peter Bryant and Lynette Bradley and studies undertaken in Sweden, Denmark, the USA and Australia. Bryant and Bradley (1985) undertook a longitudinal study with some five- to six-year-old children who had had poor phonological skills as four- to five-year-old pre-readers. The results of differential training showed that the group of children who had explicit training in sound/spelling correspondences did outstandingly the best.

The Cumbria study by Hatcher *et al*, selected four groups of six- to seven-year-old struggling readers, matching them for reading, spelling and phonological skills. There was one control group (some of whom received remedial help independently of the study programme), one group who were given phonological training alone, one who were given linked phonological and reading training and one who were given reading training but without any specific reference to phonology. The reading training activities were largely modelled on Marie Clay's 'Reading Recovery' procedures (Marie Clay, 1985).

The intervention programme lasted for 25 weeks and, as you would expect, all the children improved over this period. The phonology and reading group, however, consistently made the greatest improvements in reading and spelling. On reading accuracy, they made a year's progress in 20 weeks and their advantage was still evident nine months after the intervention had ceased. The only finding that went against the trend of phonological linkage superiority related to the reading-only group, who showed up particularly well on sight vocabulary recognition (presumably as this was what their reading-only training tended to emphasize). While the phonology-only group did particularly well on phonological tests, this advantage did not carry over into reading and spelling. Overall, the results suggested that teaching graphophonics is strikingly beneficial to reading development.

These results support the phonological linkage hypothesis. Teaching is most effective where training in phonological and reading skills is integrated. Other studies also support these conclusions. Iversen and Turner (1993) showed that a programme based on Marie Clay's procedures, but with additional phonological training, was considerably more effective than Clay's original procedures on their own. Children need to be taught how to apply their phonological skills to the challenges of reading and writing.

These findings, of course, only relate directly to struggling readers in Year 2. It would be surprising, however, if the effects could not be applied to younger children with reading problems and, indeed, to the teaching of reading in general.

But what of children with very severe phonological problems? While most struggling readers have some phonological problems, they may be helped by phonological training. But severe problems may be a different matter. Developmental dyslexia in children is generally the result of severe phonological deficits (to do, perhaps, with the processing of short duration sounds in the brain) and there is evidence that such children may not be helped by phonological training. It is not the scope of this book, however, to tackle such special educational needs.

Nevertheless, the problems that dyslexic children have as a result of their phonological deficits hint at the significance of phonological skills in normal development. Phonological skills would seem to be crucial in helping to organize children's understanding of print. The letter sequences of words become meaningful because they correspond with the sounds of the words which the children already know. While teachers need to be alert to exceptional problems, most children will respond well to an integrated phonological reading regime.

GRAPHOPHONICS AND PHONICS

How far should 'phonological linkage' be seen merely as rediscovering traditional phonics? Certainly, there is a great deal of evidence that systematic phonics teaching is more effective than approaches that eschew any phonics element. And it seems likely that this is because traditional phonics provide some of the essential elements of graphophonics. It links graphemes with phonemes.

Some proponents of phonics, such as Chew (1997), argue that learning phonics first and fast provides, in itself, virtually all the phonological awareness that is required. She argues that children do not need to be phonemically aware prior to learning phonics but can learn all they need to know about phonemes from learning phonics. In traditional phonics, the child puts phonemes together to make words, rather than taking words apart to discover their component phonemes – which is the difficult bit. Learning the phonic value of letters teaches all that is required about phonemes.

This argument, so far as it goes, has merits but it ignores at least two important issues. Firstly, it ignores the place of writing in supporting learning to read. Writing phonically inevitably involves analysing words into their component phonemes, and learning to write in this way feeds a new attentiveness back into reading (resulting, in part, from the child's reading back to herself what she is writing). Secondly, Chew's argument ignores the correspondences between larger-scale phonological units, like rimes, onsets and syllables, and their associated (and reliably regular) spelling patterns.

Graphophonics, then, is more than phonics, subsuming phonics within itself. What it does not do is see phonic decoding uniquely as the royal road to reading but, rather, as an important skill to have available and to integrate into a flexible array of graphophonic strategies.

INTEGRATING PHONOLOGICAL AND ALPHABETIC SKILLS

Graphophonics, crucially, is about the way sounds are encoded in print and how they may be decoded. Some phonological skills are only really developed as a result of learning the alphabet and beginning alphabetic reading. So not only do phonological skills help reading, but reading helps phonological skills – which in turn help reading. The phonological skills that seem only to develop in relation to alphabetical skills are to do with phonemes – the ability to segment and blend phonemes and so on. It almost seems as if some children need to *see* the separate graphemes in order to be able to *hear* the separate phonemes – just as some children may need to *see* the separate words on the page in order to *hear* them as discrete units in speech.

Certainly phonemic awareness doesn't seem to be spontaneous – it does not occur unprompted among illiterate people nor those who are literate only in non-alphabetic languages like Chinese. While phonemic awareness can be developed deliberately prior to an introduction to the alphabet, it is also developed when learning the alphabet. And, after all, phonemic awareness is only useful in its relationship to the alphabet and to the development of letter/sound correspondences.

BRINGING LETTER KNOWLEDGE INTO PLAY

As a teacher, what you can do is dependent on the level of the children's alphabetic knowledge. Letter knowledge should begin to be exploited as soon as it is learned in order to show its relevance to reading. This is equally important whether the children have learned letter names or letter sounds first. As far as graphophonics is concerned, letter sounds are the important issue but, as we saw in the previous chapter, the discussion of letter shapes should be exploited in helping the children to analyse the more familiar sight-words.

When children have learned some of the letter sounds, ask them, when looking at a word, which letters they know and encourage them to say their sounds. Then say the word for them or ask them to say it and to listen for the letter sound in the word. In this way you hope to develop the visual image of the word and support its recognition with elements of its sound. At the same time, doing this confirms the notion that the letters *say* the sounds in the word.

LOOKING AT SOUNDS – WORD-LEVEL WORK

You can begin to marry phonological skills with alphabetic skills by developing phonological activities of the kind discussed in Chapter 2, only now using written letters and words to reinforce the oral activity – for example:

✧ The teacher asks the child to articulate a written word slowly so as to be able to listen to each distinct sound, and to point to the letters she knows that say any of the sounds.

✧ The teacher says 'Look at this word "sit". Now listen for the sound (phoneme) /s/. I want you to tell me if it is the first sound (phoneme) or the last sound or the middle sound in the word. Now point to the letter that says the sound and tell me what it says.'

✧ The teacher says 'Look at these three words. I'm going to read them to you and I want you to tell me the two that finish with the same sound, then point to the letters and say the sound: "post", "top", 'rip".'

✧ The teacher asks 'What is the first/middle/last sound in the word "pig"? Now look at the word. Can you point to the letter that says the sound?'

✧ The teacher says 'Listen to this word: "bat". Tell me slowly, what are the sounds in the word? Now look at it. Point to the letters and tell me the sounds again.' Later, repeat this activity with words that include a consonant blend, for example, 'plan', 'hand' and so on.

✧ The teacher says 'Look at this word: "jam". Now take away the /j/. What have you left?' Then she says 'Look at this word "ice". Add /m/ at the beginning of /ice/. What do you get?'. Finally, 'If you put a /t/ instead of a /k/ at the end of /park/, what do you get?'

(You could use the word 'phoneme' instead of 'sound' with the children; if you have introduced it, as the National Literacy Strategy *Framework for Teaching* suggests. The children won't know they should be frightened by the word – even if you are! Note that some words work phonetically but might not always work as far as spelling is concerned.)

WORKING FROM SOUND TO SPELLING

Phonemic awareness permits the segmented sounding of words prior to translating the sounds into letters. Separating the segmentation and coding stages is helpful as a step towards employing phonic spelling in writing. Unlike synthetic phonics, the approach suggested below places first emphasis on sound-to-spelling correspondences rather than spelling-to-sound and is based on the work of Elkonin (1973). It develops (as a writing activity) one of the phoneme awareness activities suggested in Chapter 2.

HEARING AND WRITING THE SOUNDS IN WORDS

STEP 1

Choose phonically simple words, for example, 'mum' or 'dog'. For each word, draw a strip of boxes with one box for each phoneme in the word. Have available some counters so that the child can put a counter in each box. You may want to demonstrate the procedures to the child before asking her to undertake the task.

✧ Say the word slowly and clearly to the child and ask her to say it back to you slowly, noticing all the sounds she makes.

✧ Say the word slowly and clearly again, asking the child to put one counter for each sound she hears into the boxes (from left to right to match the reading direction).

✧ Now ask the child to say the word slowly while you put a counter in for each sound the child articulates.

✧ Now ask the child to say the word and put the counters in the boxes for herself.

By counting the counters, both you and the child can check how many sounds there are in the word.

STEP 2

Now work with words the child may want to spell in her writing. Repeat the procedures for Step 1, but additionally go through the procedure again, without the counters, asking 'What sounds can you hear?' For each sound the child tells you, ask 'How do you write it? What letters say that?' You can give the child any help or guidance she needs as you act as scribe, writing the letters she tells you. (You may need wider boxes divided by a dotted line to take the letters if the sound needs two letters to represent it. The aim is to move by degrees from a box per sound to a box per letter, so explain this to the child.)

STEP 3

Repeat the procedures for Step 2, but this time, for each sound, ask 'What letter would say that? Write it in the correct box.' Always make sure the child goes through the sounds in sequence.

STEP 4

Work without boxes, but still start with slow, deliberate and clearly-articulated pronunciation. Work from this directly into writing the letters in sequence.

This spelling activity can run in parallel with encouraging children to invent spellings in their free writing (discussed more fully in Chapter 7) – 'Write it as you think it sounds. I'll be able to read it'.

ONSETS, RIMES AND THEIR SPELLING CHUNKS

While spelling concentrates on phoneme/grapheme correspondences, other sorts of tasks look at larger sound/spelling chunks. Adams (1990) cites 37 rime spellings that contribute to nearly 500 words primary children are likely to encounter. There are about 50 common onsets, including the 20 single consonant onsets. Work that separates and combines or re-combines onsets and rimes helps children to start to perceive phonological spelling chunks in words. It draws attention to sequences of letters that are relatively reliable as guides to pronunciation and that represent phonological units of pronunciation that children are naturally alert to. Such chunks are relatively easy to learn and are encountered fairly frequently in different combinations in different words. Work on building up word families based on particular onsets or rimes can help. For example, a search for descriptive words beginning with 'sl-' might throw up 'slack', 'sleek', 'sleepy', 'slimy', 'slinky', 'slithery', 'slippery' and so on. This sounds like a good start for writing a poem to me!

Work on common rime patterns is, perhaps, even more useful than that on onsets. Children fairly readily learn to use the first letters of words as phonic cues, but the rest of the word is not so easily decoded. Work on rhyming rimes and the way they are often represented in common spelling sequences alerts children to the rime as a phonological and graphophonic unit at one and the same time. This is an issue we will return to in Chapter 8.

HEARING RHYMES, SEEING RHYMES, SPELLING RHYMES

Choose a nursery rhyme – but make sure the rhymes in it *really* rhyme and are spelled homographically, for example, 'Jack and Jill', but ignoring the 'water/after' quasi-rhyme. Write it out in large letters, then:

✧ read it with the children, drawing attention to the rhymes they hear;

✧ ask the children to listen for the rhymes, identify them and point to them. You then highlight them;

✧ rewrite the rhyming words under each other so that the commonality of spelling is evident:

Jill　　down
hill　　crown

✧ ask the children to provide other rhyming words, for example, 'pill', 'spill', 'fill'; 'clown', 'brown', 'town', add them to the list.

Discreetly deflect attention from any proffered rhymes that don't fit the spelling pattern!

✧ display rhyme lists (or make rhyme books) and add to them as opportunities present themselves.

PERMING ONSETS AND RIMES

It is fairly easy to devise different ways of getting the children to perm a selection of onsets and rimes to see whether they make a word the child knows. For example, consider the following onsets and rimes:

> onsets: 'h-' 'r-' 'fl-' 'ch-' ;
> rimes: '-at' '-en' '-ip' '-og'.

These will perm to give us:

> real words such as: 'hat', 'hen', 'hip', 'hog', 'rat', 'rip', 'flat', 'flip', 'flog', 'chat', 'chip'; and nonsense words such as: 'ren', 'rog', 'flen', 'chen', 'chog'.

Of course, you have to be careful to avoid the possible production of certain Anglo-Saxon words! And you may feel uncertain what to do if children consign real words they don't know (for example, 'hog', 'tat', 'tog') to the nonsense category or claim some words are real that are in fact spelled differently (for example, 'plat', 'hed'). You can say 'Yes, I would know what you meant if you wrote it like that, but in fact we spell that word a different way.' It is best to teach separate 'rules', for example, 'head', 'bread' and 'dead', on separate occasions, to avoid confusion and distraction from the main point of the lesson.

PERMING ONSETS AND RIMES

There are a variety of physical devices you can employ to align different onsets and rimes, thus helping the perming process. For example, one tube rotating inside another, with onsets and rimes written in line with the axis of rotation; two concentric rotating card wheels, with the onsets and rimes written radially on them; onset and rime lists on cards you can slide against each other to bring different onsets and rimes into combination; packs of onset and rime cards to put together in different combinations and so on.

Such card packs can be used in a variety of ways: cooperatively, assigning the permed words to the real or nonsense categories; competitively in 'Snap' or simply with all the cards laid out, and each child or team searching in turn to put a real word together.

ONSET-RIME PELMANISM

Place all onset and rime cards face down. Each player in turn picks up two cards. If they make a real word, the player keeps them. If not, he or she shows them to the other players and replaces them, face down, in their original places. The child who makes most words is the winner.

RIME-ONSET DOMINOES

Make domino card with rimes to the left-hand end, onsets to the right and, of course, a space in between. Children then chain them to make real words they can read, thus:

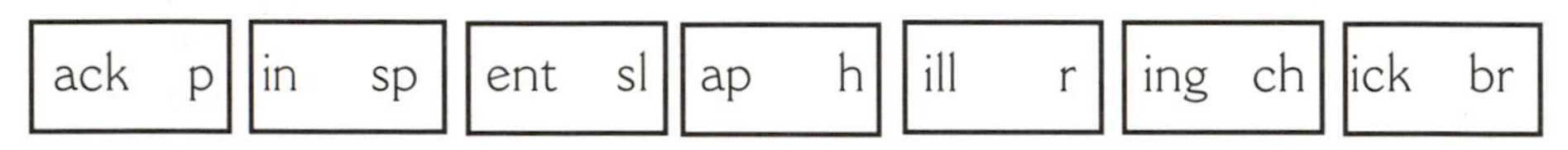

✧ Start with single consonant onsets, adding digraphs and blends as children can manage them.
✧ Extend the activity by asking children to list the real and the non-words they can make, for example, 'bring' and 'brack'.

TRANSFORMING RHYMING WORDS

In order to help children be more aware of the sounds shared by different words and how these common sounds often share spelling patterns, Bradley (Bryant and Bradley, 1985) devised the following procedure, which I summarize here:

> Ask the child to choose a short word with plenty of rhymes, eg, 'hen'. Then ask the child to spell it, using movable letters. Now ask the child to spell a word that rhymes with it, eg, 'pen'. Continue with this until the child realizes she doesn't need to scrap the previous word totally in order to spell the next, but only needs to change one letter. Extend with other rhymes or words with shared onsets, shared beginnings, for example, 'pen', 'peg', 'pet', or simply with shared vowel sounds, for example, 'pen', 'met', 'bed'.

It is a nice point as to what you do if the child doesn't realize she doesn't need to scrap the previous spelling totally – if she doesn't achieve the Eureka! experience. The teacher's task is to prompt insight. Even if you have to point out the strategy, there is still an element of insight for the child to understand what you mean. And she makes the insight her own by practising its use and adapting it to new requirements, for instance, to new words, to words including onset blends, to alliterating and assonantal words.

Hatcher *et al*, interestingly, make use of non-words for some of their activities. The advantages of non-words are that children find them fun and they won't know them, so they will have to listen to them very carefully and have to work out the spelling (or, alternatively, pronunciation). Indeed, it may give a child a particular sense of ownership to invent a nonsense word and then spell it!

CONCLUSION

Teaching children how to bring phonological awareness and alphabetic skills together is a crucial strategy in teaching reading. It should be tackled at two levels at least – at the phoneme-to-letter level of correspondence; and at the onset/rime-to-spelling level of correspondence. This kind of work on correspondences should be practised in both directions, the sound-to-symbol direction and back from symbol to sound. Such sound/symbol translations are a major topic in Part Three: Working Out Words.

CHAPTER 6

PREDICTION AND PARTIAL ALPHABETIC CUES

Children need to develop strategies for working out words for two reasons; one, because they are meeting new words all the time; and two, because they need to revise the words of their pre-alphabetic vocabulary in a more secure, 'worked-out' way. In the long run, the words in the child's sight vocabulary have to be known as fully-analysed recognition units if the child is to develop as a skilled reader.

For the child with only a pre-alphabetic sight vocabulary, there are two reading strategies available: either to try to fit the new word into an existing pigeonhole (for example, the child who read 'smaller' as 'yellow' because it fitted the two-sticks-in-the-middle paradigm – see Chapter 1) or to guess. I think we have all met readers who operate only in these terms!

There is, I suppose, also another option – refusal, simply stopping at the word, expecting help. Children who have been exclusively taught by look-and-say methods tend to categorize words as 'their' words which they can read or as 'other' words which aren't their responsibility to attempt. Hence the refusal. This behaviour is evidence that the child has not begun to develop strategies for working out words. In general, such children feel powerless in the face of unyielding print.

CONTEXTUAL GUESSING

Guessing (or 'predicting') is a spontaneous strategy that children try and, at best, it is motivated by their desire to make sense of the text they are reading. Although it is an important strategy signifying, as it does, the yet more important propensity to search for meaning, guessing has been hyped by many theorists in the last couple of decades to a more central position than it deserves. Most of what student-teachers are taught about language experience approaches, 'apprenticeship' and shared reading is predicated upon the notion of guessing or predicting – and this is at the expense of attending to decoding the written words.

Similarly, the vast majority of reading schemes designed during this period have been based upon prediction. The most commercially successful scheme, the *Oxford Reading Tree*, is one such scheme that gives meaning its top priority; meaning is seen as a means of predicting the identity of words, rather than word identification being seen as a means of discovering meaning. (At least, this was the case until recently when the *Woodpeckers* and *Rhyme and Analogy* units have shown *Oxford Reading Tree* to be reappraising its rationale!) Similarly, *Story Chest* (according to Brooks (1992) the most widely recommended scheme in teacher training) argued that:

> Reading unknown words is a prediction exercise for all readers; for the young 'early reader' it is an exciting guessing game in which they use their experience, their language, the cues from the book and the encouragement of their teacher, relative or friend to guess at the most likely meanings. By providing books which tell good stories in natural language, teachers offer children the best possible chance of making correct predictions.
>
> (Teacher's File, 1991, page 8)

Guessing can be considered a way of working out words by prioritizing meaning and context, rather than the printed words and letters on the page. We need to understand both its uses and its limitations.

'READING – A PSYCHOLINGUISTIC GUESSING GAME'

Ken Goodman (1967), whose ideas inspired these approaches, called reading 'a psycholinguistic guessing game'. Yet he did not mean to suggest that reading is a matter of blind or wild guessing. He used the term 'guessing' for its shock value, but is just as happy with the term 'prediction', which sounds much more rational! What he was aiming to draw attention to was the role of anticipation of meaning by the reader.

The developing reader does not simply decode text. Because she is actively engaged in seeking meaning, following the context of meaning and syntax, she also derives expectations from general knowledge and from what she has already read. These enable the reader to anticipate what the text is going to say next. Guessing is a matter of the reader using meaning to try to work out what the words say – or, rather, what she thinks they *ought* to say. For example, Anne-Marie (Year 3) reads:

> Mum picked up the baby from a cot beside her.

where the text actually says:

> Mum picked up the baby from a cot beside
> the bed.

It would seem that Anne-Marie's sense of how the meaning was going leaped ahead of her reading (which, perhaps, paused for a moment at the line ending). In the event, as her eyes caught up, she self-corrected. But what is clear is that, in saying '... beside her', she predicted how she thought the sentence ought to go.

Her approach here closely follows Goodman's account of the reading process. Goodman argued that the reader samples the text, decoding the minimum that allows her to predict the next word and then monitors the text to confirm that prediction, before moving on to the next prediction. If, however, the monitoring of the text disconfirms the prediction, the reader has to correct by re-sampling the text.

So, guessing isn't necessarily haphazard. As it happened, Anne-Marie's guess was not at all influenced by the letters in the word (presumably because she hadn't reached them yet), but was influenced by the context. As soon as she registered the actual wording, she was alert to the mismatch between the text and her guess, and so corrected herself.

If Anne-Marie had guessed correctly, then there would have been no mismatch, no self-correction, and no evidence at all as to which came first, the anticipation of meaning or the decoding of the print.

GUESSING PROMPTED BY ALPHABETIC CUES

Much more common than guesses that leap ahead of looking at the print, however, are guesses that are, in part, suggested by an incomplete reading of the printed word. Guessing is used as a substitute for full graphophonic processing. Some such guessing looks fairly haphazard. Thomas (Year 5) reads:

> He creeps his map.

where the text actually says:

> He checks his map.

There are some commonalities between the actual word and the word Thomas reads – the first and last letters, one vowel and the overall length of the word. And the word he substitutes is, appropriately, a verb. But it makes no sense at all. And he doesn't notice. He even goes on to repeat the error in the next sentence because he thinks he has identified the word correctly:

> He creeps all the buttons and switches.

Guessing that doesn't relate to contextual meaning, even when influenced by partial alphabetic processes, is a disaster. But even when guesses do relate to contextual meaning, they can still be unsatisfactory. Again, Thomas reads:

> First of all, he picks up two gas tanks.
>
> He drops them across to the rocket.

where the text actually says:

> First of all, he picks up two gas tanks.
>
> He drags them across to the rocket.

It seems as if the miscue is suggested in part by the first two letters of 'drags' and in part by the meaning of 'picks up' which suggests its opposite, 'drops'. Additionally, the general length and configuration of 'drags', with its penultimate descender and its final '-s', may have contributed to the miscue. What is clear is that guessing has substituted for a full reading. And the guess was probably prompted by the preceding context. But the oddity of meaning in what he reads ('drops them across to') was not sufficient to make him review his reading.

Some miscues suggested by context and partial alphabetic reading make reasonable or even perfect sense. Daniel (Year 3) reads:

> He stood behind Pete...

where the text says:

> He stopped behind Pete...

In the context, this makes complete sense. The miscue, while remaining an error, coordinates meaning and some of the information from the printed text.

There are, then, two sides to contextual guessing. On the one hand, guesses can be deemed 'good' when they are based on a sound grasp and anticipation of meaning in the text. On the other hand, when guessing is used as a substitute for paying full attention to the graphophonic information on the page (whether in partial alphabetic reading or in failing to check a prediction with the printed word), guessing is a dysfunctional strategy for the child to adopt. Reading requires that we register the actual wording of the text. Guessing can result in evading this requirement.

GUESSING AND CONTEXTUAL UNDERSTANDING

'Good' guesses show an intelligent use of context. The context operates in the reader's mind at four different levels: two relate to the context outside the immediate sentence being read, and two relate to the sentence itself:

✧ First, there is the general context of meaning of the story, perhaps an everyday story based on school experience. The child brings to the story her background knowledge and her sense of what is possible, and probable, in such a situation. A fairy story or animal story might, in contrast, permit magic or talking animals.

✧ Secondly, there are expectations derived from the language and wording of the preceding text – as when we speculated that 'drops' was suggested by 'picks up', or where a particular subject area like 'school' primes the reader to recognize particular words belonging to the vocabulary of 'school', for example, 'teacher'.

The two aspects of the immediate sentence that are relevant to context are semantics and syntax:

✧ The sentence, as it unfolds, both opens up and forecloses various possible meanings: for instance, 'When the base is about the size of a saucer, it is time to start...' From both the general context and the sentence so far, only a limited set of meanings is probable. It is easier to make an intelligent guess in the second half of a sentence than the first!

✧ The sentence, as it unfolds, makes its grammatical structure clearer. In the example given above, 'start' must be followed either by a noun phrase, for example, '... start the sides' or a present participle, perhaps, '... start building up the sides'. Children are intuitively very sensitive to these syntactic requirements and rarely offer a guess that won't fit grammatically. Syntax is a powerful, though unconscious, constraint which, if it doesn't prompt the guessing of a particular word, at least determines the probable part of speech to be chosen and any related grammatical agreements, for example, between subject and verb.

EXPECTATIONS WORK TOGETHER

In early reading, many expectations derive from the illustrations. The pictures, which a child is likely to look at first (especially if the teacher discusses the book and pictures with the child before reading begins) open up the whole field of reference of the story – animals, say, or school. Thus the child is primed to expect certain words and certain events. In well designed books, the illustrations on each page may well support the accompanying text. For example, the illustrations in *Oxford Reading Tree* are specifically designed to suggest what the predicate of the accompanying sentence will say. Thus, if the sentence starts 'Chip took...', the child can look at the picture and see what Chip is taking, and make an informed guess.

On the other hand, in some stories, for example, *Rosie's Walk* and *Not Now, Bernard*, the pictures tell a much more complex story than the words, so guessing from the pictures will not be an effective strategy. What the child is gaining from the relationship between text and pictures in such stories is something different – the beginning of 'reading between the lines', perhaps, or even a sense of dramatic irony, sharing a 'hidden' meaning.

Many traditional stories and stories written specially for children include formulae ('Once upon a time...') and patterned language, as in *The Gingerbread Man* and *The Enormous Turnip*. The use of repetition enables children to join in a telling and to anticipate the text in a shared reading. Such patterning is used to good effect in reading schemes, for example, *Storyworlds*, where in one story, the sentence, 'Tabitha was a travelling cat' recurs like a leitmotif and the child will quickly anticipate its recurrence – four to six repetitions should teach the word 'travelling'!

YOU CAN'T PREDICT THE UNPREDICTABLE

So far we have suggested that guessing is spontaneous, that it is constrained by syntax and meaning, and that it can be prompted by partial alphabetic reading. The most unsatisfactory guesses are those that are prompted by partial alphabetic reading without any contextual influence involved.

At best, contextual guessing is an intelligent way of using meaning to predict what might come next. And the best early texts for children are designed to be predictable. However, no text is wholly predictable and, as texts become more complex and subject matters more wide-ranging, they become less predictable. Open choice cloze passages rarely give rise to just one set of solutions! Guessing, in the long run, is a strategy for failure. It is only the youngest readers, or struggling readers like Thomas (mentioned earlier on page 81), who depend upon it.

THE USES OF PREDICTION

Yet intelligent anticipation, if not outright guessing, has an important part to play in reading success. It is part of the comprehension process, which will be dealt with in greater detail in Chapter 10. Comprehension is not just a matter of passively processing the information that arrives, but involves actively seeking it. At this point, however, we are not concerned with overall comprehension, but with how seeking meaning, which is what prompts guessing, contributes to identifying words.

Firstly, it primes the processing system with expectations, facilitating word identification. Secondly, it works in cooperation with partial alphabetic processes, as when the child sounds the first letter of a word and then guesses, *and then checks the guess against the complete printed word*. Such a guess is constrained by initial sound, plausible meaning and grammatical acceptability. For example, consider the full story of Daniel, where he read:

> He stopped behind Pete…

rather than:

> He stood behind Pete…

The guess had to satisfy three criteria: it had to include certain identified letter elements, for example, the initial 'st-', the final '-d' and the '-o'; it had to be an intransitive verb in the past tense; and it had to be something a teacher might well do in a classroom. Of course, put like this, it sounds an impossibly complex conundrum. But these constraints operate at an intuitive level. Words offer themselves for inspection... and there are only a limited number that might fit.

In the event, after saying 'stopped', Daniel corrected himself. Even after guessing a word that fitted for sense, he wasn't satisfied until the word both made sense and fitted the full spelling. His semantic system, like Anne-Marie's when she said 'the cot beside her', was running ahead of full visual processing and, like her, he had a cross-checking strategy in place to coordinate information from both semantic and graphophonic processes. In the end, if the reading is to be accurate, the contextual guess always has to defer to the written word.

TEACHING AT THE PARTIAL ALPHABETIC/GUESSING STAGE

The teacher's task is threefold at this stage:

- ✧ the teacher has to promote comprehension and intelligent prediction – which includes cross-checking guesses for meaning in context;
- ✧ the teacher has to encourage cross-checking guesses with the spelling of the printed word;
- ✧ the teacher has to facilitate the development of swift and full alphabetic processing so that, ultimately, the visual identification of words is faster than semantic processes.

Teaching for comprehension, like facilitating full alphabetic processing, will be dealt with more fully in later chapters. It is sufficient here to say that you may feel it appropriate, when listening to a child who is only just coming to terms with alphabetical processes, to prompt 'sound the first letter and guess' strategies. *However, always follow up the guess by asking the child to look at the word and check whether the guess was right.* When listening to children read, it is appropriate to challenge them over meaning or word identification if they read something incorrectly by asking 'Does that make sense? No? So look again'. Or, where appropriate, 'What you've just read makes sense. But did it really say that? Which word did you get wrong? Check it now. How does this word begin? And the word you said, how does that begin?'

PARTIAL ALPHABETIC PHONICS

The child need not initially be asked to attempt the whole phonic procedure all at once. The teacher may begin by asking the child merely to sound out the first letter of a problem word. Perhaps he or she judges that all that is needed is a phonetic prompt to remind the child of the problem word – perhaps a sight-word that should be familiar. Or perhaps the target word is new and irregular, and the teacher judges that a phonetic prompt and the context will help the child make a suitable guess.

Teachers' judgements may be based on two considerations. Firstly, partial alphabetic reading normally precedes full alphabetic reading (unless the child has been taught phonics-first), and the child will not, at first, be expected to synthesize the whole word. She may not yet even have learned the whole alphabet. Children regularly use even partial knowledge where they can. Secondly, if the child is reading a story, new words don't crop up in a total vacuum without any contextual support. The grammar of the sentence gives syntactic support and the story (including the pictures) gives semantic support. These kinds of support activate expectations about what might come next.

The teacher has an array of strategies to prompt the child into partial alphabetic reading:

✧ If a child is stuck on a word, the teacher may prompt a guess by re-reading the sentence up to the target word, leaving the rhythm of the sentence dangling invitingly open, hoping this sort of contextual prompt may mesh with some incipient alphabetic decoding.

✧ If the guess is incorrect and makes no sense, the teacher may say, 'Listen to what you have just said,' and repeat what the child has just read. 'Does that make sense? Let's look at the first letter and see what it says.'

✧ If the child guesses incorrectly but the guess makes some sense in context, the teacher may say, 'Yes, that makes sense. But look at the first letter of the word. What sound is it? Does your word start with that sound?'

✧ If the child guesses correctly, the teacher can say, 'Well done. Yes, look at the first letter of the word. That makes the first sound in what you said. Say it again, what is that first sound? Show me the letter that says it. Now let's look at all the letters. Do you think you will know the word next time?'

✧ If the child cannot hazard a guess, the teacher may ask the child to sound the first letter as a prompt to contextual guessing.

✧ If the child cannot sound the first letter, then the problem probably lies further back – the child is not secure about letter identification or letter sounds. The teacher can tell the child the word and the letter sound and ask her if she will remember it next time – and make a note to do more alphabet work with the child.

What the teacher is encouraging here are two elements: using phonic sounding out to prompt a contextual guess, and checking a guess against the phonic evidence. This is the beginning of the vital strategy of cross-checking between graphophonic and contextual sources of information, which is a step towards the child becoming self-monitoring and self-teaching.

It is, perhaps, important to point out that the teacher's prompting strategies given above are not an exhaustive list. Further strategies are discussed in Chapters 8 and 11. The teacher should nudge the child in the direction of strategies that are appropriate to the target word in question and to the child's stage of development.

GUESSING AS AN ATROPHYING FUNCTION OF COMPREHENSION

Although children can guess intelligently and can check the guess against the printed word, guessing (or predicting) is a strategy of limited value and no real long-term use except in artificial situations like cloze passages or dealing with half-illegible texts. What underpins the capacity to guess, however, remains important. The ability to guess depends upon active comprehension, an interactive 'dialogue' with the text, with the reader constantly constructing and reconstructing meaning in the light of what she is reading, assimilating and accommodating new information as she goes. Active comprehension is more important and of vastly more long-term significance than its offshoot, the ability to guess.

As the reader becomes more able and fluent, word

identification becomes swifter than anticipation. The cross-checking function, which initially worked one way round at the partial alphabetic/guessing stage, comes to operate the other way round. A guess is no longer checked against the print, but the word identified from the print is checked for meaning – does it make sense in context? The adult reader's monitoring system is not so much a matter of checking whether the written words correspond with predictions, as of being alert to meaning, so any anomaly in meaning triggers the reader to reprocess the text.

CONCLUSION

Guessing is a strategy that comes easily to children and, at best, it represents the exploitation of intelligent anticipation of meaning to make up for a weakness or slowness in the graphophonic identification of words. Children spontaneously develop a strategy of partial alphabetic reading supported by guessing, and teachers often promote the strategy by encouraging children to sound out the first letters and guess, when they are stuck on a word. The teacher has to ensure, however, that: the guesses are grounded in an understanding of the preceding text; the guesses are then checked against the spelling to ensure their accuracy; the child studies the spelling to help ensure recognition of the word in the future.

CHAPTER 7

ALPHABETIC READING AND PHONICS

FULL ALPHABETIC READING

Full alphabetic reading takes the whole spelling of a word into account. It processes all the letters in sequence in order to establish what the word 'says' and thence, from its pronunciation, to identify it. This is a procedure that can be used to identify new words, but the same sort of processing applies, if less consciously and deliberately, to familiar sight-words.

Alphabetic processing doesn't happen automatically but can be encouraged if:

✧ the teacher directs specific attention to the spelling of a word and inculcates a general attitude of attentiveness to spellings and shared sequences between words;

✧ the child is taught to process the word graphophonically;

✧ the child writes the word, working it out rather than copying.

These experiences combine to make the reader know the word more thoroughly.

Analysing a word alphabetically is not only a matter of working out how it sounds but also of using its sounds as a way to organize and understand its spelling. It is through alphabetic processing that the two-route model of word recognition, discussed in Chapter 1, begins to take shape.

In the early stages of alphabetic reading, the building blocks from which word sounds are synthesized may primarily be individual letters or digraphs. But at the same time, the phonological units that the child is naturally alert to (rimes, onsets, syllables) will tend to map onto the patterns of spelling that correspond to them and facilitate their being perceived as visual units. For example, rhyming rimes (for example, /ick/,

/ight/) tend to draw attention to their common spelling patterns ('-ick', '-ight') and make them visually memorable.

Because these spelling units, like letters, marry within themselves both a visual and a phonological identity, they are graphophonic units. As time and teaching go on, these graphophonic spelling chunks emerge as recognition units. Such developments will, however, be the subject of the next chapter. This chapter is largely concerned with how words are built up from letter sequences and identified from their pronunciations – the territory of traditional phonics.

TRADITIONAL PHONICS

Systematic phonics teaching has been found to benefit children with a limited pre-school background in literacy, struggling readers, children with special educational needs and dyslexics among others. Nevertheless, it raises strong views, both for and against. Let us try to consider its educational effectiveness dispassionately.

REASONS TO BE PRO-PHONICS

Phonics help to establish:

✧ the phonemic values of the letters;

✧ the discipline of left-to-right serial scanning;

✧ the discipline of giving attention to the whole letter-string of a word;

✧ sounding-out and blending procedures for tackling new words, and as a fall-back strategy;

✧ the notion that graphemes may involve more than one letter, so spelling *patterns* start to be identified;

✧ phonic spelling strategies – which incidentally reinforce directionality and phonemic awareness.

REASONS TO BE ANTI-PHONICS

✧ phonics doesn't teach children to think about the meaning of what they are reading, only to translate print into sound;

✧ phonics doesn't work because English spelling is too irregular and if you ensure that the words children meet are all regular, this inevitably means children only get to read inane texts;

✧ teaching phonics is a slow process that fails to motivate;

✧ phonics may promote dead end, mechanical decoding routines that interfere with the development of a sight vocabulary and preclude the development of orthographic chunking and so on.

While there are strong arguments both for and against phonics, most of the negative ones mentioned here can be obviated by thoughtful teaching. If we teach phonics *within* reading, rather than teach reading exclusively by phonics, we can have the best of both worlds.

PHONICS FIRST AND FAST?

Proponents of phonics (for example, Chew, 1997; McNee, 1996; Turner and Burkard, 1996) advocate teaching phonics first and fast. While this is possible, there are good reasons against doing so. Not least, that it ignores the experience children bring with them to school and their natural propensity to search for meaning themselves. First-and-fast phonics is a matter of programming children with procedures and it can lead to children feeling that they aren't reading properly if they are not sounding out each word. It makes them distrust any other ways of identifying words, including ones that exploit their own intelligence and creativity.

Nevertheless, the procedures of phonics should be a major weapon in the child's armoury for word attack. They provide a confidence-building strategy for coping with new words. And beyond phonics procedures, phonic knowledge has a wider role, if a harder one to define: it facilitates the development of orthographic recognition units, the 'chunking' of spellings into significant pronounceable units.

A BALANCED USE OF PHONICS

A balanced approach teaches phonics in parallel with whole-word strategies and with other graphophonic strategies. The aim is gradually, as alphabetic knowledge becomes established, to introduce phonics as a progressively more thorough-going word attack skill. At the same time, it is exploited as the initial way for children to tackle spelling in their writing.

Such a parallel approach is not all plain sailing. Oakhill and Garnham (1988) argue:

> ... although a whole-word approach may get the reader off to a good start, there is bound to come a time when a more analytic approach is required. (page 88)

> ... beginning readers should not be started on phonics straight away, as such a difficult approach may well alienate them from reading. (page 101)

However, they conclude, following Chall (1983), that intensive phonic training first and fast is better than *intrinsic* training where phonics is introduced as an ancillary support after reading has been embarked upon through whole-word sight recognition. Can we resolve this apparent contradiction?

The resolution lies in system and flexibility. While phonics concentrates on one model of mapping sounds onto spellings, children who have been shown variable letter/sound mappings from the start, learn new material better. If we can teach children to use sounding out and (say) rime recognition together to help identify a word (for example, /s-t-r-ing/), we may have cracked it.

Oakhill and Garnham recommend teaching an initial sight vocabulary and gradually introducing phonics only when the children are reasonably confident. They suggest starting to discuss sound/spelling correspondences through rhyming and spelling-identical chunks, and working other correspondences downwards through compound words, syllables and finally phonemes – much the pattern suggested here, except I want to run synthetic phonics more in parallel with chunking, rather than working down to it.

SYSTEM IN PHONICS TEACHING

Different phonics schemes suggest different orders for tackling the graphemes and have different notions of what spelling rules should be included within a reasonably comprehensive coverage. While such schemes can be useful to the teacher as points of reference, what research seems to suggest is that there should be a close match between explicit teaching and the texts upon which the children are going to practise, confirm and develop their new skills. This rather suggests that the teacher will need to adapt the teaching content to the vocabulary of the reading schemes available.

Rather than setting up a blueprint, then, it might be more appropriate to think in terms of checklists and outcome assessment. Checklists will ensure coverage of things like consonants, consonant digraphs, consonant blending, short and long vowel sounds, and vowel digraphs including the separated 'magic *e*'. What neither a checklist nor a systematic phonics programme can do is cover *all* the hundreds of spelling rules! Much, inevitably, must be left to the child to work out in her own practice.

An assessment of outcomes is a matter of checking what skills and strategies the children actually use. Are they confident and competent in applying phonic knowledge to solve problems in reading – that is, in tackling new words, seeing patterns in spelling and assimilating new words to their sight vocabulary? Do they systematically tackle new words by employing a variety of skills and strategies at the same time – contextual cues, phonic word building and analogies with known words – but give priority to the graphophonic processes? The outcome we want is one where the child has sounding-out routines available for use but doesn't use them routinely, using them only for problem solving, confirming the identification of words and ultimately consigning such words to a fully-processed sight vocabulary.

DECODING WORDS USING SYNTHETIC PHONICS

This is perhaps the nub of phonics. It is the systematic application of phonic knowledge to achieve the phonemic translation of the word by sounding out the letters and blending the sounds. The term 'synthetic' refers to this building up of a word sound by sound and blending (synthesizing) the sounds into an approximate pronunciation.

Synthetic phonics is appropriate:

- ✧ only with regularly spelled words or words that are largely amenable to phonics;
- ✧ initially, at any rate, with words already in the child's speech vocabulary;
- ✧ when the child can recognize the letters instantly;
- ✧ when the child can produce the letter sounds instantly;
- ✧ when the child knows to proceed from left-to-right through the word;
- ✧ when the child can recall and blend the sounds in sequence;
- ✧ when the child can listen to her own pronunciation (at first aloud; later, perhaps, silently) and identify a real word from this approximate word sound.

All this, while sounding a bit daunting, is perfectly feasible. Chew (1997) cites the example of children reading the word 'school' in the Schonell Graded Word Reading Test:

> Phonics-taught children who had not yet learnt about the hard Greek 'ch' might at first pronounce the 'ch' as in 'chop'...but three phonemes out of four would be right and the children would often spontaneously correct their pronunciation of the fourth. (page 182)

She provides data showing that four- and five-year-old children taught phonics systematically and matched for Schonell reading age with six-year-olds taught by mixed methods, performed very much better on reading new, phonically-regular words.

Nevertheless, many children do have problems with synthetic phonics. Clay (1991) observes that children do not resort to sounding out spontaneously. Bussis *et al* (1985) found that, of the children in their study who had received systematic instruction in phonics, fewer than half actually used sounding-out and blending procedures with reasonably consistent success:

> The blending of sound segments was simply not a very workable strategy for the majority of the children, and their problems with it were numerous. (page 97)

Three problems stood out:

✧ a failure to recognize the words that had been sounded out, even when the blending produced a fair approximation to the sound;

✧ a tendency to reversal or transposition in the phoneme sequences – they cite the example of one boy who couldn't manage the name 'Stan', producing 'Sant' and 'Sans' even after being told the word (remember 'spaghetti', Chapter 2?);

✧ children were thrown by the unreliability of phonic rules, for example, problems with 'put'.

Particularly striking were problems that emerged where the phonic rule is itself honoured as much in the breach as in the observance. They cite difficulties with the digraph 'ea', where one boy pronounced 'feast' as /fest/ and 'already' as /alreedy/, showing the total confusion caused by an unreliable rule. These children don't sound as if they would have coped with 'school' in the way that Chew's children did! McNee (1996), however, to obviate this problem, simply suggests teaching children to try the /ee/ pronunciation of 'ea' first, and if it doesn't make a real word, to try the /e/ pronunciation.

PROBLEMS WITH BLENDING AND RECOGNITION

Typically, with early readers who have been taught to apply phonics, sounding out operates at a speed of about one letter per second. Normal pronunciation operates at roughly ten to fifteen phonemes per second (Pinker, 1995). With such differences in timing, the child is unlikely to perceive the sounded phonemes flowing together as a word. Blending, as a separate stage from sounding, speeds up the pronunciation to something closer to a normal pronunciation rate where recognition of the word becomes more likely. In order to blend the sounds, however, the child must recall them in serial order and say them, smoothing them out as much as possible into a fluent pronunciation.

This pronunciation may well only be an approximation of the correct one for many reasons: the pronunciation of many consonants is difficult without adding a vowel sound, for example, /buh/, /duh/; the pronunciation of a given phoneme is not a fixed quantity but adapts to the phonemes either side of it on account of the way the mouth, lips and tongue move to anticipate what is needed to pronounce the next phoneme. Add to this the fact that until the reader knows what the word is, she cannot know the right rhythms and stress pattern to apply: for example, until you know that 'carrot' says /carrot/, you can't know that the last syllable doesn't say /rot/, but something more like /rut/ (nor, for that matter, that the first syllable doesn't say /car/!). As a consequence, the blended pronunciation of the separate phonemes may be lumpen and misleading.

The whole phonic process is not without its problems, but it sometimes works as a last resort. And it is probably employed by reasonably able readers, *sotto voce*, more often than Marie Clay allows. She recommends giving children time to work words out, and this is quite probably one of the ways they do so.

TEACHING SYNTHETIC PHONICS

Teaching synthetic phonics is a follow-on from alphabet work, partial alphabetic strategies and oral phonemic synthesis. It can be taught as a whole-class or group activity within the Literacy Hour. While it has to be taught very deliberately, since it doesn't seem to develop spontaneously, the teacher must bear in mind that it is not the only effective way to tackle a word; and it is not always an appropriate way – for instance, with irregular words.

When demonstrating and practising sounding out and blending routines, start with those words which the children already know. This way, they can see how the system works. Then move on to unknown – or even invented – words closely analogous to the words you began with. Invented words are fun for the children to make up and they specifically test phonic strategies because there is no other way of tackling them.

Particular care will be needed with initial consonant blends as there is some tendency in the auditory memory, between the initial sounding out and the blending, for children to rearrange the order of the phonemes to split up the blend (see the problem with 'Stan', discussed above). Children can, to some extent, cope better with final blends – perhaps because they have more experience of them unitized within a rime. Final blends, as separate items, are perhaps best approached through rime families: for example, it is better to approach '-st' after having looked at '-ast', '-est', '-ist' than to try approaching the rimes through the blend. This may not seem a very pure and logical way of doing phonics – but who ever suggested the child's mind works in a pure and logical way? If alertness to rimes is more natural to the child than alertness to phonemes, then it is appropriate to teach using rimes.

However systematic our approach, we cannot cover everything. Approaches based on the vocabulary demands of reading schemes may work just as well as more sophisticated systems. We pick up or work out a good deal of phonics for ourselves as a result of reading experience. At the moment, Jessica (Reception Year) reads the 'a' in 'a dog' like the 'a' in /apple/. But there is little point in teaching, as some phonics systems do, the indeterminate vowel sound found in words like 'better', 'again', 'a present' and so on. It would be too complex. She will naturalize her pronunciation in her own good time. Meanwhile, the apple /a/ is good for most short words a child will encounter. The point of teaching is to develop a strategy to add to the child's strategic repertoire, not to make a phonic zombie of her!

TEACHING THE LETTERS TO TALK

RECAP LETTER SOUNDS

First you need to check that the children are secure naming and sounding the letters you are going to use in the words you start with, so that the letters *can* talk. Use letter cards for this.

USE CHILDREN'S NAMES

Make a game of identifying children's names. Choose someone's name and write up the letters one by one, asking the children to give you the sound of each one, then going back to the beginning each time to sound it out up to the point you have reached. Children will guess the name at some point, if they don't recognize it straightaway. Ask them to tell you the next sound to write and to check if what you actually write fits in with their guess. When it is all written out, sound it out together and blend it.

USE SOME REGULAR SIGHT-WORDS THE CHILDREN KNOW

Tell them the word and start to write it out. Ask the children to sound it out a letter at a time, proposing a letter then checking and so on.

DEMONSTRATE SYNTHETIC PHONICS

Say 'Here's a way to read words you don't know.' Demonstrate sounding out and blending, asking the children to try to identify the word from your vocalizing (note that this extends from the oral blending games discussed in Chapter 2).

WORD-BUILDING FROM LETTERS

Show letter cards to check they know the sounds, then assemble them into words. Put the letters out in turn, with the children sounding them. Then, when the word is complete, the children blend the sounds. Start this with known words, but you may also use non-words – 'If there was a word like this, how would it sound?' You can develop the game by rearranging the letters to give different words, for example, swapping the first and last letters so 'pat' becomes 'tap' and so on.

SYNTHESIZING REGULAR WORDS (INCLUDING NEW WORDS)

Present this as a challenge. If the children can read the word, they collect it; if they can't, you collect it and whoever gets most wins. (Of course, make sure they win!) Insist on the steps of sounding out, blending and recognizing. To ensure that the children are not depending on prior knowledge and recognition, you can introduce obscure or non-words, but warn them first.

For these procedures, choose words that use the short vowel sounds only to start with – as in 'ham', 'hen', 'fin', 'fox', 'fun'. The initial consonant sounds, as far as possible, should be ones that do not carry vowel additions – such as, 'f', 'h', 'l', 'm', 'n', 'r', 's', 'v', 'z' and so on. This will give you the chance to point to the letters while saying the sound. Final consonants are not so crucial in this respect.

INTRODUCING NEW GRAPHEMES OR CONSONANT BLENDS

If the digraph, blend or 'magic *e*' occurs in a reading scheme word, look at that word together. With a vowel digraph, explain the rule, for example, 'When two vowels go walking, the first does the talking'. With a consonant digraph, add it to the alphabet. With a consonant blend, get the children to 'unpack' the constituent phonemes. In all cases, ask the children to propose other words that work the same way (but don't confuse the issue by discussing ones that don't work). Write them under each other so that common spelling patterns show clearly. With multi-letter graphemes, highlight the grapheme to unitize it, for example, showing the 'magic *e*' at work.

USING PHONICS IN READING

Phonics is not strategy for indiscriminate use – you want the children to know words by sight rather than to work them out afresh every time they meet them. Even with regular words, a full phonics procedure is not the only way for a child to work out a word, though some elements of phonics are going to be involved in other approaches, for example, sounding the onset and guessing or using rime analogy. Even irregular words contain phonic cues that can act as mnemonics to support sight-learning them – especially if you play 'silly pronunciations' with them like /y-a-ch-t/. Some, of course, behave in regular ways when you consider their rimes as a unit, for example, 'all', 'ball', 'call' and so on. Other words show different patterns, such as, the 'wh-' words like 'who', 'why', 'where', 'when', 'which' and 'what'. Then there are less coherent groups like 'was', 'want', 'what', 'watch' and 'wallaby'. There are two things to say about these kinds of words. One is that there will always be something about them that can act as a phonic clue. The other is there will generally be a group of words that work in the same irregular way, making their own regular pattern. Talking about where the spelling 'goes funny' can help make it memorable.

CHANGE-A-LETTER WORD CHAINS

VERSION 1

The teacher shows a word to the children and asks them to read it. Then he or she writes another word beneath it with a one letter difference, so 'net' becomes 'not'. The teacher asks which letter has been changed, the first, middle or last, and what it says. He or she then writes another word beneath, perhaps 'hot'. After the children have got the idea, the teacher can ask for their suggestions for the next word, and so on.

VERSION 2

This is played by two children. It can be played with movable letters or with a pencil and paper. If using movable letters, the children will need to record which words they make. The game is cooperative, with the children trying to make as long a chain as they can. One child starts with a three-letter word, the second child has to read it, and then write a word of her own, one letter different, for example, 'pig', 'big', 'bin', 'bun', 'but', 'hut', and so on. Good chains can be used in class phonics lessons and be turned into a classroom display.

INVENTED SPELLING

Many eminent writers believe it is more beneficial to start phonics with *invented* phonic spelling rather than with phonic reading. Writing is a letter-by-letter activity and lends itself to the practice of phonic skills, although the child needs to analyse words into phonemes, which is difficult. However, phonological activities like slowed-down pronunciation and the phoneme counter counting game (see Chapter 2) can help.

Carol Chomsky (1979) noted that children who invent their own spellings when writing 'receive valuable practice in translating from sound to print', which is 'an excellent basis for reading later on', and which encourages 'a do-it-yourself attitude which carries over into learning to read.' Clay (1991) says that one of the benefits of invented spelling is that

> ...many children may not need phonic instruction once they acquire and use a sound sequence analysis strategy.
>
> (page 85)

Encouraging children to work out spellings for themselves helps them to understand how spelling works and how reading works. They tend to write more (uninhibited by 'correctness') and become avidly curious about print. Adams (1990) suggests that the enhanced performance of invented spellers results from 'their own, necessarily thoughtful and active efforts to spell'. Clark (1976) says the benefits are particularly significant for children who come to school with a weak reading background, showing both in better spelling and better word recognition.

TEACHING INVENTED SPELLING AND 'CORRECTNESS'

As soon as possible, the child should be encouraged to try to work out spellings independently, even if the spellings are not standard. You can start out by saying, 'Spell it how you think it sounds'. Usually you will be able to interpret what the child means – you simply have to read the words phonically, remembering the child sometimes uses the letter sound, sometimes the name. Thus 'ppl' represents 'people'; 'r' represents 'are' or 'our'; 'cr' represents 'car'; 'craen' represents 'crying'; and 'jriv' represents 'drive' and so on. The important thing is to value the efforts and the writing and not to give the idea that 'correctness' is more important than meaning. We need to show our appreciation and understanding of the child's efforts. What the children gain is both a grasp of phonic sounds and sequence and confidence in their own problem-solving capabilities.

Correct spelling develops from reading and gaining a visual sense of how the word should go. For example, you are more likely to come across 'wos' than 'woz', though the latter is more phonetic. This is because, in such a common word, the visual pattern, in which first and last letters are more salient than internal letters, contributes to the invented spelling. With wider reading experience, the child develops a visual memory for the patterns in spellings and will want to get spellings right. 'Sound-to-letter analysis does not reign supreme...for very long' (Clay, 1991). The very skills the child learns through invented spelling alert her to correct spellings: invented spelling is a self-correcting process, accelerated by reading experience and the separate teaching of spelling patterns. Invented spellers become the best spellers because of the kind of attention they have learned to give.

CONCLUSION

Alphabetic reading and phonics are concerned with processing all the letters in a word in their sequence and interrelations. The processing is a matter of translating the spellings into pronunciations in order to identify the word. This letter-by-letter approach only works completely successfully with regular words, though all words, however irregular, contain phonic cues that can help with their identification. While the processing procedures of sounding out and blending can be taught, they do not come easily to children, and the method is not best considered as an initial teaching method, but as one strategy among others. In some ways, it tends to act as a fail-safe or backstop method for coping with new words. At best, it analyses the spellings of new words and dispatches them, fully analysed, to the sight-word memory as recognition units.

Phonic spelling comes more readily to children than phonic reading and the approach to spelling it induces has a spin-off for reading. Between them, they encourage a way of perceiving and processing spellings that assists in establishing the fully-processed sight vocabulary that characterizes successful readers.

CHAPTER 8

FROM PHONOLOGICAL TO GRAPHIC CHUNKING

One of the central processes in the development of reading skills is the development of chunking – that is, learning automatically to perceive the letters in words as grouping themselves into orthographic recognition units. These units are known and pronounceable spelling sequences. Some are whole words, some are parts of words, for example, syllables like '-tain' (contain, maintain and so on), rimes like '-ack' or inflections like '-ed' ('washed', 'cooked' and so on).

A compound word, first learned perhaps as a pre-alphabetic or partial alphabetic word, may come with further experience to be seen as a two-part word – for example, 'Postman Pat' may well be recognized initially in context as pre-alphabetic sight-words, but with more alphabetic experience 'Postman' may be seen as 'Post + man'. Inflected words may similarly be analysed visually as two-part words. Daniel (Year 3), for example, read the word 'friends' by stages: 'fr... friend... friends'.

First he tackled the onset as a chunk, 'fr-', then read the basic word or stem, 'friend'. Then he self-corrected, re-reading it as 'friends'. He had *seen* the word 'friend' as a unit or chunk, and then seen and responded to the suffix '-s'.

In chunking the word as 'friend + s', he had chunked the word into its constituent morphemes, or units of meaning. Frith (1985) argues that, as reading develops, 'orthographic units ideally coincide with morphemes'. As adults, we typically chunk words into constituent morphemes – even when making mistakes! For example, recently I misread 'seesawing' as 'sees-a-wing' – three perfectly good morphemes! Whether you chunk 'organize' as a whole word or as 'organ + ize' is hard to be certain – but you will certainly identify '-ize' as a verb ending. And you have to chunk 'organizing' as 'organiz(e) + ing', the stem and the present participle marker, in order to understand how the word fits grammatically into its context.

Adult chunking develops out of the processes that begin in the child. Initially, however, children's chunking is based on phonological chunks rather than morphological chunks – though, of course, the two can coincide, as with the '-ing' ending.

THE BEGINNINGS OF CHUNKING

Ehri (1995) cites research that shows a significant difference between First and Second Grade readers in their grasp of chunking. When undertaking word searches, First Graders were sensitive only to words they knew, whereas the more experienced Second Grade readers were sensitive to the difference between permissible sequences and impermissible sequences of letters. These children were not dependent, like the First Graders, on identifying a word they knew, but could identify spelling patterns that could plausibly make a word they didn't know.

In this way, the spelling 'traw' is permissible, but 'triw' is not. Between known words and letters, there develops a range of recognition units which are not necessarily words in themselves, but are potentially parts of words (as with '-aw' above). Spelling permissibility is closely related to pronounceability.

Bussis *et al* (1985) cite the example of a boy called Tim (First Grade) who, after reading several pages without error, got stuck at the word 'know'. Eventually the teacher had to tell him the word. Later, reading a more difficult passage, Tim got stuck on the word 'grow'. When asked to sound out the initial consonant blend, he came out with a whole word, 'great'. After other unsuccessful attempts, he said, 'If there were an 'n' there, I would know.'

The teacher asked what it would be if there were an 'n' there. Tim said, 'Know.' Then he explained, 'The 'r' wouldn't be there; the 'n' would be there.'

The teacher asked, 'And what would the first letter be?' Tim answered, 'A 'k'.' The teacher, understanding at last, improved the shining hour, saying, 'Oh! So you are talking about the word *know*, huh? Okay, maybe this rhymes with *know*. Could you make it rhyme with *know* but start with *gr*?' Tim suggested, 'Grow?' The teacher exclaimed, 'That's right – good job!'

Bussis *et al* remark that in general his miscues reflect (faulty) attention to spelling patterns rather than (faulty) attention to letter/sound correspondences. What is striking about the anecdote is that while Tim cannot manage sounding-out routines, he has a visual memory of spelling patterns which he can use for making mental comparisons. He doesn't volunteer a rime analogy and the query after he says 'grow' suggests he is not confident about it. But he is equipped to move in this direction.

PHONOLOGICAL CHUNKING

The phonological units the child is most immediately alert to are whole words, syllables, rimes and onsets. It is in terms of these units that the chunking of spelling initially takes place. This chunking depends upon a certain level of alphabetic skill, since the child needs to be able to recognize letter sequences.

Such chunking seems, in principle, to operate in the opposite direction from synthetic phonics. Synthetic phonics works from phonemes upwards, via blending, to words. Chunking works from phonological units downwards, via mapping, to perceiving spelling patterns as pronounceable recognition units.

PHONOLOGICAL UNITS AND 'RIME STABILITY'

In theory, when children learn words as pre-readers, an auditory image of the word and a meaning become associated in the mental lexicon. The auditory image is composed from the minimal phonological units they are alert to – namely onsets and rimes. So if early readers are learning about mapping sounds onto written language, it should be easier to map onsets and rimes onto spellings than to map phonemes onto letters.

To add to this theoretical possibility, there are certain facts about spelling which are significant. Individual letters, especially vowels, are not reliable guides to their pronunciation. The pronunciation of vowels tends to be influenced strongly by the letters immediately following them. Consequently, the spellings of rimes are fairly reliable guides to their pronunciations – including their vowel sounds. For example, each of the letters 'i', 'g' and 'h', on its own, is phonetically ambiguous (*cf.*, 'kit' and 'kite'; 'gum' and 'gem'; 'house' and 'hour'). But together as '-igh', they constitute a pretty reliable guide to pronunciation. Usha Goswami (1995) calls this pronunciational reliability 'rime stability'.

The notion of rime stability is confirmed by Seidenberg and McClelland's (1989) computer model of reading. The statistical relations between letter sequences and pronunciations confirm the reliability of rimes for predicting the pronunciations of new words. This suggests that experience which includes paying full attention to spelling sequences may well make rimes particularly significant features for decoding print into pronunciations.

So, what does all this amount to? In relation to rime spellings, we find that children are alert to phonological rimes and that rimes are fairly reliably represented in spellings. We have the potential here for a more reliable mapping of sounds onto spellings than we have with synthetic phonics. This theoretical possibility is confirmed in practice in ways reminiscent of Tim's tentative 'know/grow' analogy discussed earlier.

RIME ANALOGY

Over the last ten years or so, Usha Goswami has explored the ability of children to make graphophonic analogies. In particular, she has shown that children can read new words by analogy with known words, using rhyme as the linking element. In one experiment, she presented children with a 'clue-word' that was new to them and told them what it said. Then she showed them other words that shared certain elements of spelling and pronunciation with the clue-word. For example, using the clue-word 'beak', she tested children with words like 'bark', 'bean' and 'peak' – words that all shared two phonemes with the clue-word. Children consistently proved better able to use the information from the clue-word to read rhyming words than non-rhyming words. For example, 'beak' led to reading 'peak' and 'weak' but not to 'bark' and 'bank'. (There was some tendency to be able to read 'bean', but not as much.)

A similar effect was found using words with alliterating onset blends, but this effect was not as strong as with rhyming rimes. The children seemed to be making analogies based on graphophonic inferences – if 'peak' looks like 'beak' then it will sound like it. The argument extrapolates that children can be self-teaching, using rime and onset analogies. One almost feels, reading Goswami and Bryant (1990), that inferences like these are the magic key to reading!

Ehri (1995) reports related findings. Six- to seven-year-olds with some decoding skills were taught to read one set of words. Then they were required to learn a second set. For one group, the second set of words contained the same rime spellings as the first set of words (for example, 'feed' – 'seed'). For the other group, the second set of words employed the same letter/sound correspondences as the first set, but without the same rime spellings (much like Goswami's test words). The children learned to read the rime-analogous words faster than the non-analogous words. Ehri, interested in consolidated alphabetic reading, concludes that:

> ...shared letter patterns facilitate the process of remembering how to read words, that is, building a sight vocabulary. (page 122)

She doesn't mention that the rimes rhymed, though this is evidently the case. Her findings suggests that chunking spellings according to phonologically salient units helps learning.

TEACHING PHONOLOGICAL CHUNKING THROUGH ONSET AND RIME ANALOGY

There is now a great deal of published material available to help in this area. Goswami's findings have had a direct effect on contemporary reading materials. Rhyme and rime analogy elements are being introduced by the major publishers. Goswami has herself written the Teacher's Guide for the *Oxford Reading Tree*'s excellent 'Rhyme and Analogy' strand.

Consequently, here I shall simply signpost certain principles, together with examples of supporting activities and strategies.

1. **Play with rhymes and onsets orally and demonstrate their common spelling patterns visually,** for example, develop ideas suggested in Chapter 5 about exploring rhymes in poems, avoiding rhymes that are embodied in non-homographic spelling patterns (for example, high–sky, wool–full):

✧ Ask the children to compose the spellings using movable letters.

✧ Orally compose new poems modelled on the original, perhaps using the names of children in the class:

Jake and Jane went on a plane
To fetch a cup of coffee.
Jake fell out and gave a shout,
"Please, throw me down a toffee!"

✧ Write and compare the rhyming words.

2. **Develop alertness to onsets and rimes and their possible permutations in word-making,** for example, using the rime-onset dominoes (see Chapter 5). Develop it further by asking the children to make further cards themselves to add to the pack. This can be done by taking a real word and splitting it, or it can be tackled by thinking of onsets and rimes in isolation.

3. **Teach and practise the strategy of using analogies to identify words,** for example, playing clue-word games.

A clue-word is any word you choose to represent a particular productive rime, for instance, 'nest', which can generate 'best', 'chest', 'jest', 'pest', 'quest', 'rest', 'test', 'vest', and so on.

CLUE-WORD GAMES

✧ Display the clue-word, perhaps with a supportive picture, and either ask the children to read it, or tell them what it is.

✧ Ask the children to make the word from movable letters.

✧ Ask the children to tell you a word that rhymes with the clue-word. Discuss what bit of the clue-word rhymes. Introduce a slight gap between the onset letters and rime letters to make the rhyme clear.

✧ Ask the children to sound the onset of the clue-word and then to sound the rime.

✧ Now spell out the rhyming word the children chose in letters beneath and aligned with the clue word.

✧ Ask them to read the rime. It is visibly the same as the clue-word so ask them how they did/might use the clue-word as an analogy.

✧ Ask them to sound the onset (they can consult the alphabet frieze or you can help them if they are struggling).

✧ Now ask the children to sound the onset and the rime, that is, to read the new word (they should recognize it as the rhyming word they chose).

✧ Explore other words that rhyme with the clue-word.

✧ You can emphasize spelling by asking the children to spell the rhyming word they chose, using the clue-word as a guide. In the process, encourage them to tell you how they are using the clue-word as an analogy.

✧ As the children become more fluent in this task, you can leave steps out, approaching something closer to the test procedure – presenting the clue-word(s) and trialling new words (including non-words).

✧ You can undertake similar activities using alliterating onsets.

4. Support the children's use of analogy in reading and writing by providing visual rime and onset clue word displays for reference, for example, by making a rime tree.

MAKING A RIME TREE

Goswami (1996) suggests making a reference display:

✧ Make a tree with five main branches, one for each of the short vowel sounds. Label the branches.

✧ After each clue-word session, or whenever a discussion about a particular rime has taken place, place the clue-word on the appropriate branch, according to the central vowel sound in the rime.

✧ Categorizing by vowel sound is useful because it draws attention to the vowel (often the last sound to be attended to). You teach the children to use the vowel to locate a clue-word to enable them to find an analogy which will help them with either reading or spelling.

✧ You will need more branches or a new display for long vowel sounds, for example, those based on vowel digraphs.

GRAPHIC AND MORPHEMIC CHUNKS

The first chunking that children adopt is based on phonological mapping. But other mappings also develop, based on patterns of meaning although always with phonological support. These are the patterns that the National Curriculum highlights under the heading 'graphic knowledge', largely in response to the work of Bussis *et al* (1985), who noted that:

> ... as the children progressed in reading skill, most of them... evidence(d) knowledge of the spelling and grammatical meaning of frequently encountered word parts. By "word parts", we mean common affixes appearing at the beginning or end of a word... (page 104)

Such affixes include 'un-', 'pre-', '-s', '-tion', '-ed', '-er', '-est', '-ly' and so on.

What is significant about their observations, beyond simply the issue of part-word chunking, is that these chunks constitute morphological units. Morphology is the study of the elements in words that carry meaning, both semantic and syntactic. A morpheme is a unit carrying a single element of meaning. Thus the word 'television' is composed of two morphemes, 'tele +

vision' meaning 'distant + seeing'. Single letters can also be morphemes, as with the '-s' that makes 'friends' plural.

Frith (1985) saw the development of identifying morphemes as, perhaps, the culminating step in reading development – which makes sense, if reading is about gaining meaning. Byrne (1998) found that pre-literate children tend to focus on the morphemic or semantic function of letters (for example, the pluralizing '-s') to the exclusion of their phonemic roles. In this light, much of the value of phonological chunking could be seen as being to facilitate the development of morphological chunking.

Affixes (prefixes, suffixes, inflections) all carry elements of meaning. As word parts, they are readily identified because they have phonological identities, grammatical significance and they remain constant, added variously to different word-stems.

Word stems also have phonological identities and remain constants to which variable affixes can be attached. Some stems are words in themselves, for example, 'see', which gives us 'sees', 'seer', 'unseen' and 'seen'. The suffixes here indicate what part of speech (verb, noun, adjective and so on) each word might be: and each affix indicates the same qualification of meaning in many other words (such as, 'painter', 'undo'). The child reader intuitively starts to put these regularities together, building up a vocabulary of meaningful word parts.

Many morphemes are complete words, not part-words, indivisible with regard to meaning, for example, 'apple'. But for reading, the significance of morphology is that it provides a unitizing principle for chunking parts within complex words.

Morphology is an element in grammar and children have an implicit sense of grammar that precedes, and develops alongside and in response to, their reading. Attentiveness to morphology helps the reader interpret the syntax and meaning of a text – as Bussis *et al* remark:

> Since affixes signal grammatical meanings, the children's knowledge of these orthographic units strengthened their ability to anticipate the grammatical structure of text.
>
> (page 104)

Specifically, it is suffixes, including the inflected endings of verbs, that signal grammatical meaning. Bussis *et al* cite the example of Jane who typically, when she misread a complicated word, gave it an ending that was grammatically appropriate: for example, she misread 'discovery' as 'discoveration', 'magisterial' as 'magisterly'. She clearly knows (at some level) that '-ation' signals a noun and '-ly' an adjective, when added to a noun. Sensitivity to syntax is evident in children, according to Marie Clay (1991) and many others, from halfway through their first year of reading instruction.

Bussis *et al* noted that some children paid attention to spelling patterns from the very beginning of their reading efforts. Although they often had difficulty employing synthetic phonics, their phonic knowledge facilitated their alertness to the spelling patterns of affixes, their pronunciations and the grammatical categories established by suffixes. The majority of children in the Bussis study gave attention to affixes as they became more proficient readers:

> They seemed to construct a store of 'sight affixes' in a somewhat analogous fashion to the way they had constructed a nucleus of 'sight-words' at an earlier stage of reading... The children's knowledge of affixes proved to be a much more versatile and useful resource for negotiating difficult text than their previous sight vocabulary.
>
> (pages 105–6)

Of course, the children still had a whole-word sight vocabulary – they didn't unlearn the words they had learned at an earlier stage of reading! But what their part-word vocabulary shows is that they have acquired a chunking strategy that can be used flexibly to identify words. They are beginning to see words and part-words as unitized spelling chunks. And the corollary of this is that they start to see complex words as constructed from meaningful chunks added together.

One result of learning alphabetic strategies is that spelling patterns cohere as unitized symbols for pronunciations. An early unitizing factor is phonology, as we saw with rimes, but morphology constitutes another unitizing factor. Morphology reinforces phonological units, giving them additional significance. These recognition units are not just inscribed in graphophonic processes, but they are also inscribed in semantic processes.

TEACHING GRAPHIC READING SKILLS

Teaching about the composition of complex words can be conducted at an explicit level. The grammar underpinning word endings can largely be left implicit – we explore questions of grammar by appealing to intuition and by asking if it sounds right. But we can talk explicitly about the composition of compound words, the patterns of inflections required for agreement in sentences, about the common features of meaning reflected in different prefixes and suffixes and, with older children, we can talk about stems, roots and etymology.

Nunes (1998) suggests that inventing words from combining stems (for example, inventing names for new dinosaurs) and working out the meanings of words invented from novel combinations of stems and affixes (for example, to 'unclimb' a hill), help children to learn a framework for thinking about language and morphology.

As far as reading is concerned, such explicit attention aims to have implicit effects, an 'attunedness' to perceiving patterns that relate spellings and meanings, and an ability to separate stems and affixes mentally to assist word identification.

This attunedness is something that develops spontaneously in reading. It is for the teacher to encourage and develop it and to be alert to it when listening to reading. Since much of the significance of the morphological part-words is to do with grammar, and grammar is largely intuitive, making much of these elements analytically may be unproductive. But exploring patterns and inventing words can be fun.

(Wasn't 'attunedness' a lovely word? I invented it, following affixative rules. And isn't 'affixative' a lovely word! I've just invented it, too – and you've understood it, because you know the affixes and the rules, as well!)

In listening to reading and helping with problem words, the teacher should be ready to prompt the child, where appropriate, to separate the stem and affixes, if this helps word identification. As far as direct instruction in reading is concerned, many of the elements are best approached in the first instance simply as phonological units, for example, '-ation', and exploration of its morphological significance come later.

ACTIVITIES TO SUPPORT GRAPHIC KNOWLEDGE AND CHUNKING

CLOZE PROCEDURES

Cloze passages may be prepared with affixes in general, suffixes or inflections left blank. Each of these options focuses on something slightly different. For example, prefixes left blank will draw attention to the composition of complex words, as with:

> There were some _____ordinary animals in *Jurassic Park*.

Suffixes left blank focus more on syntax and agreements, as with:

> He was draw____ on the wall when the teach___ came in
> and shout___ at h___.

MAKING AND BREAKING WORDS

The same general procedure can be used here as with certain onset-rime activities. Cards can be prepared in two sets: one of stems and one of suffixes, including inflections. A stem card is turned up, for example, 'teach'. Then a suffix card is turned up, possibly, '-ed'. 'Teached' is not a word, so no score. But if '-er' is turned up, 'teacher' is a word, so the child scores. But note:

- at first, care needs to be taken that the spellings don't need modification as suffixes are added;
- later, stems can be used where spellings will need to be adapted, so 'run' becomes 'running', 'fly' becomes 'flies'. Extra points can be gained for correct spelling adaptations.

WORD SEARCHES

Beyond alertness to graphic chunks, children need practice in perceiving meaningful or, at least plausible, spelling sequences at a glance. Word searches require the child to spot meaningful sequences amid a lot of distractions, so they are exercising the unitizedness (nice word!) of a child's knowledge of word spellings and permissible spelling patterns.

✧ Start with horizontal only displays, such as,

p e l a m b i
u f o s i n g

(Additional vertically displayed words come later.)

✧ Extend the activity to include listing non-words that obey the rules of permissible spellings: so in the above example 'pelam' and 'fosing' are permissible. The children can be asked to explain their decisions by providing spelling analogies, such as, 'posing/fosing', or discussing pronounceability.

CONCLUSION

Adult sight reading is a virtually instant identification of words from known spelling patterns – either the spelling of the whole word or of the meaningful chunks that combine to make the word. Such consolidated alphabetic (or orthographic) reading, then, depends upon the development of chunking, identifying complete spelling patterns instantly as recognition units.

Chunking is facilitated by full alphabetic reading – attending to all the letters in their sequence. But chunks initially become unitized as the result of familiar phonological units (syllables, onsets, rimes, affixes) being mapped onto spellings. Such mappings are reinforced by the frequency of certain letter sequences appearing in different words and being regularly associated with specific pronunciations. One way teachers can exploit this phonological mapping is to teach the use of rime analogies as a strategy for decoding new words.

Many of the chunks identified by phonological mapping are reinforced as they prove to have morphological significance. Thus, the '-ing' word ending is not only a phonological rime unit, as in 'king', but is a syllabic morphological unit, for example, in 'walking'. Children in Key Stage 1 begin not only to learn to read whole-word spellings but also acquire a vocabulary of word parts – perhaps especially of word endings and inflections – that have morphological significance.

Teaching should aim to encourage the development of chunking by promoting the association between spelling patterns and spontaneous phonological chunks like syllables, onsets and rimes. It should also draw attention to repeated spelling patterns and to the notion of permissible spelling sequences. The way to do this is by discussing complex words, prefixes and, more particularly, suffixes, including inflections; and by drawing attention to word composition and decomposition as appropriate while listening to readers.

CHAPTER 9

LITERAL COMPREHENSION

We read in order to understand what's been written. That seems straightforward enough – yet understanding what's been written isn't an entirely straightforward process. There are a lot of aspects to be considered. So far we have primarily been concerned with processes of word identification, but to be able to understand what we are reading, we must:

✧ put the words together into meaningful sentences;

✧ choose the relevant meaning of each word in the light of the overall trend of meaning of the sentence;

✧ remember the gist of the sentence long after we have forgotten the actual words;

✧ respond to how the wording and meaning of the sentences link together in a chain of developing meaning;

✧ make inferences to link and interpret meanings not made explicit in the text and fill out details in the light of what we already know, both about the text so far and about life and literature in general;

✧ integrate the information from the text, our background knowledge, and the assumptions and inferences we have made, into a conceptual schema and commit it to long-term memory;

✧ monitor our own processes to be alert to whether or not we have understood what we are reading.

We can think of understanding, then, as operating at the literal level of what the words say, mediated by grammar, and the inferential level of reading between the lines and interpreting what is said in terms of one's own experience.

First, I want to consider the literal and inferential levels together, to show how they relate to each other in a reading. Then the rest of the chapter will deal with understanding at the literal level, and the next will deal with the reader's contribution in terms of inference, elaboration and response in the light of her knowledge and experience.

WHAT DO CHILDREN HAVE TO DO WHEN THEY ARE READING?

Consider this passage from *My Cat Sam* (from *Supersonics: Fun with Phonics* by Ginn):

> Sam is a black cat,
> an I-like-a-snack cat,
> a drink-at-the-sink cat,
> a gone-in-a-wink cat...

The teaching notes advise the teacher to read the text aloud to the children 'taking care to allow the rhythms of the verses and the rhymes to catch the ear', before the children are asked to read it themselves. Reading it aloud will also help the children *hear* the flow of the language and how the grammar fits together.

This is important, because the grammar is complex. Each of the lines 2 to 4 consists of a complex noun phrase which you can consider either as an alternative complement to 'Sam is...', or as a phrase in apposition to 'cat' in the first line. Each phrase contains a complex modifier (adjectival phrase) with the words linked by hyphens. In line 2 this modifier is itself a complete clause, 'I like a snack'. In the next two lines, the modifiers are phrases that include adverbial prepositional phrases... I am only going into the grammar of the sentence in this way in order to show how complex it actually is. The child will need to hold all this information in her head in all its internal relationships in order to understand the sentence – she will need to understand the clause 'I like a snack' but also understand it as a part of a description of the cat, where the 'I' refers to the cat, not to the speaker of the sentence. All this puts quite a strain on the child's grammatical grasp and working memory. Nevertheless, with the help of the teacher's reading, the child can do it. Indeed, the whole book has such verve, I can imagine children wanting to learn it off by heart!

The grammar is not the only level of challenge in the passage. There is a challenge at the level of the experience of life – well, at least of cats – that the child brings to the text. A 'drink-at-the-sink cat' is first cousin to the Rum Tum Tugger who 'only likes what he finds for himself': but you have to know cats to appreciate this! The pleasure of the book derives in a large part from relating the text to one's personal experience of the contrariness of cats and one's social/hygienic knowledge about the undesirability of allowing cats to drink at the sink and eat anything that's going!

How might a child's understanding of the text show itself? A four-year-old might say, 'I'm going to buy that cat. He's a naughty cat, isn't he?' Thus, the child might express an appropriate response indicating loving indulgence – and, *inter alia*, comprehension at all kinds of levels including empathy and behavioural judgements.

Such comprehension may well be supported by the pictures. But is it any the worse for this? Not if the understanding of the meaning helps the child with understanding the language and the grammar. It is through understanding contextual meanings that we learn to interpret new or difficult grammar and expressions.

PUTTING THE WORDS TOGETHER

Children have to expect what they are reading to make sense – they have to want to make sense of it and actively search for meaning. Motivation and expectation are involved here. We have all come across children, particularly boys, who seem to interpret reading simply as a task of mollifying teacher, in which they identify words without much interest or expectation that the words will make sense! We have a role here in encouraging active interest and comprehension – in part, by providing material they *want* to read.

To be able to put the words together into a meaningful sentence, children need to remember them long enough to do so – hence the practice of re-reading fluently after a stoppage. The words are held in the short-term or working memory. The speed with which words are read is important for enabling them all to be available together in the working memory. If decoding is slow or shaky, it takes up capacity in the working memory, limiting the space available for comprehension processes. Additionally, with slow reading, memory of the wording decays before the whole sentence can be processed, again limiting the possibility of comprehension.

The working memory can hold only a limited number of items at once to work upon. Adults give the impression of being able to hold more in working memory because they readily chunk the meanings of phrases and clauses into units that operate as single items in the memory, but young children are less able to effect such chunking, and tend to hold individual words as items. The result is that sentences may be longer than their memory capacity and so they can't readily survey the whole sentence as one. They cope with this by operating various strategies, including using meaning and expectation to supplement word retention, and working according to certain simplifying rules of thumb in relation to grammar. These rules include:

✧ assuming that sentences will follow a simple sentence form, such as the indicative subject-verb-object form;

✧ assuming that the words nearest each other relate to each other (sometimes called 'the proximity rule').

An instance of the way simplifying assumptions and the proximity rule operate occurs often with 'wh-' questions:

> Q. Why did they all want to live with her?
>
> A. Yes.

The child has answered the simpler 'Did they all want to live with her?' question. This question is contained verbatim in the 'wh-' question, and it makes sense on its own without having to seek farther back in the sentence for words which may already be slipping below the horizon of memory. And the simpler question form also requires a simpler answer!

One aspect of the working memory is the 'articulatory loop' which extends its capacity for retaining words by storing them as internalized pronunciations. At the same time, the words are processed grammatically to establish how they fit together. These processes combine to produce the intonation pattern of the sentence that highlights its structure and information content.

Even very young children have patterns of grammatical expectation about how words should go together – as we have seen, usually in straightforward, simple subject – verb – (object/complement) – (adverbial) patterns, as in, 'She pulled her hand out of the box,' and 'You're safe!'

However, the limitations of their working memory capacity and experience with condensed information content and complex grammar may cause children problems. As experienced readers, adults are better at chunking sentences into manageable grammatical and semantic units. Children can get lost in longer or more complex sentences. For example, the first story in *Fiction 2, Longman Book Project*, includes the sentence:

> In the whale's tummy
> with bits of their boat all broken up
> were Bill and Bianca
> washing about!

A simpler version of this sentence would be 'Bill and Bianca were washing about with bits of their boat all broken up in the whale's tummy.' This would restore the subject – verb – adverbial order and, in addition would make the pronoun 'their' an anaphoric reference (that is, back to something already mentioned) rather than the much more difficult cataphoric reference (forward to something not yet mentioned). In the sentence quoted, the reader has to hold the meaning of the word 'their' in suspense until the words 'Bill and Bianca' are reached to find out who 'their' refers to, and has to restore the subject – verb order. The grammar seems gratuitously dislocated.

However, the reading on the audio cassette that accompanies the book is excellent, and the rhythm and intonation make the sentence meaning clear. Whether, for the reader, however, intonation helps with working out the grammar or depends on grammatical interpretation is uncertain. Some children can read aloud mechanically, one word at a time, and still understand what they have read, while others can read with apparent fluency and understand or remember very little. Nevertheless, in general, one-word-at-a-time readers tend to have problems with comprehension because they don't follow the grammatical and conceptual links of what they are reading – and the less it all hangs together, the less they can remember. Intonationally fluent reading that points up grammar and meaning generally indicates understanding.

THE IMPORTANCE OF READING STORIES ALOUD WELL

There are many good reasons for reading stories aloud: some are social, about sharing and enjoying things together in order to create a supportive and cohesive classroom climate; some are to do with moral and emotional issues, to inculcate sensitivities and common values; and some relate to developing comprehension. In this chapter I'm only going to consider this latter point, and only in relation to fairly literal understanding of the text.

When you read aloud you read with expression – that is, you supply the rhythms, junctures and intonation patterns that help the listener interpret the grammatical and informational structure of each sentence and the links between sentences; and you dramatize your reading to make it lively, funny or exciting. It is largely through listening to stories that children learn to make sense of new and more complex grammatical structures and other aspects of more formal or literary language, as well as gaining an overall grasp of a story.

It is usual to stop and question the children from time to time about the story. This questioning may be to ensure that the children have understood some expression, have picked up a significant point about the plot or people's feelings, or to encourage them to interrogate the story in useful ways: 'So what do you think it was like for Bill and Bianca in the whale's tummy?' 'What's happened to their boat?' 'Do you think they'll ever get out again?' Only the second of these is a literal question, answerable directly from the text. It is designed to check whether the children have understood the grammar and what has happened. Questioning should never be allowed to become an interruption to the story. Its task is to remind (especially in the case of a serial story), clarify and re-focus attention, anticipation and suspense.

Audio cassettes cannot give support by questioning, but certainly can help with comprehension and decoding skills through the fluency of the reading – if the child is following the text.

CHOOSING THE RELEVANT MEANING

While the sentence is held in the working memory, we select, nearly always unconsciously, the relevant meanings of words. The context seems to choose for us:

She pulled the laces tight and made a bow.

He stood in front of the queen and made a bow.

Of course, this example deals with *different* words that *look* the same. But the principle applies also within the range of meanings that single words can have:

the changing rooms	a good shot
the changing colours	a good degree

While a sentence is made of words, there is a sense in which the sentence determines the appropriate meaning of the words. Or, rather, *we* determine them in the process of seeking to maximize meaning.

With a child who is *not* putting meanings together and for whom, therefore, there is no context, it will not always be clear what meaning has been ascribed to a word. She may not ascribe very much meaning at all, if a story is read word by word like a word list reading test. If you suspect this, it is another occasion for prompting questions – questions about the meaning of the sentence or passage, rather than the meanings of individual words.

Comprehension can be adversely affected by not understanding the vocabulary or by accessing word meanings slowly. Training in relevant vocabulary can improve children's understanding of individual sentences, but it doesn't help with wider aspects of comprehension like integrating the meanings of different sentences or making inferences. Nevertheless, vocabulary knowledge and comprehension are closely associated – perhaps because it is overall comprehension that teaches us the meaning of new words (or new meanings of old words) in the context of a meaningful text.

REMEMBERING THE MEANING AFTER FORGETTING THE WORDS

When we are reading, the wording of each new sentence sweeps the words of the previous sentence out of the working memory. What we remember is the meaning, not the precise wording. Many studies show that people, after reading a passage, cannot tell sentences they have read before from different sentences conveying the same meaning. This kind of evidence shows that we remember meanings rather than the particular words that originally conveyed the meaning. Nor do we distinguish between the explicit meanings of the text and the assumptions and inferences we made about its meaning while we were reading it. We forget the words, but hang onto the meaning we have constructed, based on the words and the assumptions and interpretations we made while reading them.

RESPONDING TO THE LINKS BETWEEN SENTENCES

Putting the meaning together not only means putting the words together in the sentences, but also means understanding how the sentences add up to make an overall meaning.

TEXTUAL COHESION

There are, perhaps, three aspects to linking between sentences. One is lexical, the other two are conceptual. By lexical, I mean the way specific words are used in one sentence to refer back to a previous sentence. Consider the following example:

> Ellie took off her shoes.
>
> The girl lifted her feet up. Ellie took off her shoes.

Granted, the second example is ambiguous – whose shoes? But the fact that you can be uncertain shows that 'her' could (probably does) refer back to the girl, not Ellie; and that means back to the previous sentence. Not only pronouns but other lexical elements, such as sentence-openers like 'However,' or 'On the other hand,' or repetition of words or references (as we shall see), indicate how two or more sentence meanings are intended to cohere in a single, overall meaning. This linking between sentences is called 'textual cohesion'. Children can find following such links difficult – they can easily lose track of pronouns, for instance, not remembering to whom or what they refer.

THE GIVEN AND THE NEW

One kind of conceptual link between sentences works by adding new information step-by-step to the text. Each sentence starts from the 'given' and tells you something 'new' (that is, new within the text). Then the next sentence will tend to refer back to, or assume, that information, but now treat it as the 'given' (or already known) and use it as the stepping stone to the next 'new'. For example, consider the following (from 'The Magic Pencil', Collins *Pathways*):

> Gretchen went on her way. Soon she met a man digging a field. It was hard, slow work.

'Gretchen' is the *given* of the first sentence, and what we learn about her is that she 'went on her way'. The pronoun 'she' is the *given* in the next sentence (referring back to 'Gretchen' in the previous sentence). The *new* information is '... met a man digging a field'. In the third sentence 'It', which is the *given*, is a pronoun – but what noun does it refer back to? In fact, it doesn't refer back to a noun at all, since what it refers to is the digging. But the word 'digging' in the previous sentence is not a noun but the present participle of a verb. So what the pronoun 'It' refers to is not a noun in the previous sentence, but to the concept about digging that was part of the *new* in that sentence. It is not only *words* that link between sentences, but *concepts* that link in a chain of developing meaning.

Further, in this case, the reader has to infer from the meaning what part of the *new* is being referred to. 'It' doesn't refer to 'field', though that was the last noun mentioned. 'It' is the digging. We know this because another form of cohesion is in operation to make it clear: we are told that 'It' is 'work', so this refers back to the digging (which is work) and not 'field' (which isn't!).

If all this seems complex, be impressed! When listening to speech, children are generally managing to cope with it all the time, without even having to think about it! It is only in the relatively slow processes of early reading that children may fail to make the links. Reading the story to the children before asking them to read it themselves will help. And getting the children to re-read stories helps them to read more fluently and to be able to concentrate more on meaning, once the decoding problems have largely been sorted out.

OPEN AND CLOSED QUESTIONS

Asking questions is both a way of checking on children's comprehension and of prompting them into understanding. There are two kinds of questions you can ask children to check on understanding and to model for them the kinds of things they should be picking up for themselves. We can ask literal, closed questions such as, 'What was 'slow, hard work?', 'What happened to Bill and Bianca's boat in the whale's tummy?' which have *closed* answers, ie, they have single, right answers, and what they demand is a literal grasp of the text. These are asked to ensure that the children are following the narrative and to highlight significant turns in the plot. There's nothing wrong with literal, closed questioning – so long as you don't think that it is the be-all and end-all of teaching comprehension!

Open questions are those that don't necessarily have a right answer, for example, 'What do you think Bill and Bianca felt when...?', 'Why do you think Gretchen drew the picture of an ox and plough?' These kinds of questions ask for responses, judgements, interpretations. They demand that the child should have thought about the action in the story and related it to her own experiences and understandings. One reason why we often couch such questions in terms of 'What/why do you think...' is to indicate to the children that we want their ideas, and not answers from the text.

CONCLUSION

In this chapter we have considered the literal level of comprehension. The child needs to be able to identify the words of a sentence quickly enough to be able to hold them in the working memory while the grammar and word meanings are being processed. This process is one of making a conceptual model of the meaning that can be remembered even after the words have been forgotten. But the words, or at least some of them, need to reverberate long enough in memory for sentence-to-sentence links to be made, to help in the process of building up a progressive model of events in the story. Listening to stories can help children to follow complex grammar and, together with facilitative questioning, to construct a schema of the meaning.

CHAPTER 10

THE READER'S CONTRIBUTION

This chapter continues the theme of Chapter 9 about how children construct meaning while reading. But in this chapter the emphasis falls on the reader' s contribution – not on how the reader construes the words and sentences, but what the reader brings to the text in order to make sense of it.

THE CONTRIBUTION OF PRE-EXISTING KNOWLEDGE

We make sense of things in terms of what we already know. In general, we do this more easily with the help of 'advance organizers', things like looking at the pictures, the title, the blurb, or in the case of information texts, chapter titles and sub-headings: things that activate our existing framework of knowledge. Mentally, we are primed and ready.

In introducing things to children, we try to provide a mental context. We say, 'I'm now going to read you a story about pirates. Who knows something about pirates?' It is part of our stock-in-trade with any new material to remind children of what they already know before we begin.

CONTEXTS AND SCRIPTS

When we read, the text quickly creates its own context. If we meet the words 'treasure', 'cutlass' and 'plank', this language sets up contextual expectations. These expectations can involve knowledge about how people behave in specific social situations, and this sort of knowledge is sometimes called a 'script'. For example, we have a script about 'walking the plank'. Consider the following:

> The children were tied up. 'Fetch the plank', Blackbeard shouted.

> The galleon hit the rocks and water started pouring in.
> 'Fetch a plank,' Blackbeard shouted.

Different contexts, different scripts – and different uses for the plank!

The mental pictures, situations and feelings we have conjured up depend upon our prior knowledge, and they are our own mental pictures and feelings and nobody else's. We each read a different story because we have interpreted and pictured the story in ways based on our individual experiences. But we also read the same story because we have all been shaped by the same culture and share a common fund of knowledge and expectations.

INTERPRETING AND FILLING OUT MEANING

We don't just extract meaning from what is on the page. We make inferences, we elaborate on it from our own knowledge, we link it to what we already know. Many studies have shown that we cannot, in retrospect, distinguish between what was explicitly written in a text and the inferences and interpretations we made while reading it.

Inferences operate at many different levels. Consider the following (from 'The New Baby', Collins *Pathways*).

> It was half term. Kulbir Bedi and his Dad waited at the railway station for Grandma... The train stopped with a hiss of its brakes. Kulbir watched all the doors as they opened. There she was! (page 2)

At one level, we infer from his name that Kulbir is from a South Asian family. But less obvious are some of the other inferences we make without thinking about them.

Did Grandma come by train? Did she get off the train? Of course she did! But it doesn't actually say so. We infer that she did, and we are able to do so because we know about waiting and trains and doors and stations and visits. We have a schema or 'script' we can refer to that helps us fill out information that isn't made explicit. And we do this automatically and unconsciously.

We can go even further in making inferences. Was Kulbir glad to see his Grandma? Of course he was – but how do we know? It has something to do with 'family' scripts, 'meeting' scripts and that exclamation mark! It is also connected with our own feelings about grandmas – the writer makes assumptions about our shared emotional, as well as physical, experience.

One of the more important uses of inference in reading stories relates to feelings and motivation – how does someone feel? Why does he or she do something? Such inferences are to do with empathy with that person's situation, based on how you would feel yourself. It is a vital part of both the pleasure and the education of reading. Consider the following (from 'Sticks and Stones', Collins *Pathways*):

> "Stinky little Frogface," Jean called after Anna.
>
> "Stinky little Frogface," shouted Jean and Sharon together.
>
> Anna began to run. Kim crossed the road, but that didn't stop Jean.
>
> "Pongy little Ping Pong," she yelled.

What did Anna feel and why did she run? Why did Kim cross the road? Though the clause '... but that didn't stop Jean' implies Kim had hoped crossing the road would stop her, it doesn't tell us why she wanted Jean to stop. In the end, these questions can only be answered in the light of our own feelings and experience.

INTERROGATING THE TEXT

The story *Sticks and Stones* raises bullying as an issue, but even more immediately, it raises the questions, 'What's going to happen next to Anna?' and 'What, if anything, is Kim going to do about the situation?' It is alertness to these kinds of questions that constitutes 'interrogating the text'.

One important point to notice about the questions is that they have psychological and ethical implications. As a teacher, your task is to prompt children into 'reading between the lines' and this involves alertness to implicit feelings and motivations, and to moral issues.

The notion of 'interrogating the text' is an important one. Frank Smith (1986) talks about comprehension as being 'a matter of asking questions' of the text and 'getting these questions answered'. You continue to read in the light of these questions. You read on because you *want to find out* what happens next: you read on *in the expectation of answers*. Interrogation is a dialogue with the text that keeps you reading and thinking.

Margaret Meek (1990) says:

> ... we have to be clear that meaning is what counts... Getting the words right is only a step to reading, not reading in itself. The next move is to interpret or interrogate the text so as to go on to ask, "Do I believe that?" or "Do I like these people?" or "How do we know that?"
>
> (page 150)

These are 'higher order' questions belonging to the response/reflective/evaluative end of the spectrum of comprehension. They don't represent 'the next move' after getting the words right. Inference, elaboration, empathy and getting the story straight come first. Indeed, Meek (1988) herself suggests that it is only when the structure of the story is familiar that children are free to ask:

> What would I do if I found myself in that situation? Do I or do I not care for people like that? Is there a part of me that understands them?
>
> (page 29)

TEACHING INTERROGATION TECHNIQUES

There are questions to ask *while* reading and reflective questions to ask *after* the story has been read. The point, in interrogating the text while reading, is to focus in on suspense, the feelings and motives of the characters, your feelings about the rights and wrongs of the situation and people's behaviour. And the story itself guides us in this, as we saw with *Sticks and Stones*. Reflective questions deal with seeing the story whole, thinking about the issues it raises and evaluating the whole experience.

Questioning during reading involves:

✧ sharing suspense, for example, Is it worrying, scary? Why? What might happen? What do you want to know about? What might the character do? What can the character do?

✧ asking questions in terms of the story, for example, How does the character feel? Why do you think they are doing it? What do you think Kim (in *Sticks and Stones*) might do?

✧ asking questions to promote children's imagining themselves into the story situations, for example, How would you feel if... ? What would you do if you were Kim?

✧ asking about behaviour – What were Jean and Sharon doing? Was it kind? Was it fair? What ought Kim to do?

Reflective questioning after reading involves:

✧ reminding children of the main outlines by asking leading questions, such as, What happened to Kim on her way home from school? What did she do? What happened in the end?

✧ asking open questions that elicit personal responses to generate discussion, sharpening children's awareness of their own responses and enriching appreciation, for example, Which bit did you like best? Were there any bits when you felt worried? Was it fair when... ? How do you think they felt when... ? How did it make you feel when... ? What did you think about the behaviour of... ? Do you think what happened at the end was right? Why?

✧ asking questions about parallel life experiences – Have you ever been called names? How did it make you feel? Have you ever seen anyone else being bullied? Are these situations you should discuss with teachers, parents?

✧ encouraging children to dramatize the situation, or improvise a similar situation, to explore feelings and motives and even what the characters might do next. You might also 'hot seat' the characters in role to ask about their motives and feelings and what would be fair.

✧ evaluating the story by asking – Was it good or enjoyable? Would you recommend it or read it again? What was good about it? Are people really like that? What was it about? Have you read anything like it before, or about the same issues?

UNDERSTANDING STORY SCHEMAS

Stories tend to follow this general pattern:

Some initial situation
is disrupted by an event or challenge
which requires the main character(s) to act
to restore some kind of equilibrium.

The story ends when equilibrium is restored, though the final equilibrium is not just a return to the initial situation, but a development from it, even possibly a reversal, as when Jack and his mother end up rich ('Jack and the Beanstalk'), or where Cinderella marries the Prince. We don't aim to get children to grasp an abstract story schema like this, but we want them to be able to recall the main lines of the story in a way that makes the shape of the story clear.

We might, however, introduce the schema for *writing* stories, giving the children a pattern of prompts about creating a situation and characters, about the problem or challenge that starts things off, what the main character does about it, and how it is finally resolved. After using the schema, children might be able to think about stories they read in the same terms.

COMPREHENSION OF STORY

A good story raises emotional issues that are vital to our own life experience, presenting them in terms of situations in which the characters have to make decisions about behaviour. And, as readers, we are in the position of both empathizing with the characters in their situations and making judgements about their behaviour. Stories, in this way, provide opportunities for us to contemplate possible experiences and evaluate our feelings and judgements in relation to them, and thus they act as a vital means by which cultural and moral values are transmitted.

Talking with children about the stories they have read should enable you to judge how far the child has 'lived the story' and to evaluate the child's understanding; and it should help the child to clarify and reassess her responses while sharing her enjoyment and experiences with you.

COMPREHENDING INFORMATION TEXTS

We want children to perceive and remember the main lines of what they have read but not necessarily to have a literal recall of every detail. Traditional comprehension questions tended to focus on literal recall of details, but what we want is for the children to get the overall picture.

Well-written information texts are structured to assist comprehension in their use of layout and headings, contents pages, indexes and so on. Children have to be introduced to these structuring devices, as well as being given a reason for using them – possibly for reference, for information or for instruction. One of the main things to learn is that you don't always have to read the whole book and that you don't necessarily start at the beginning!

You do, however, have to learn to find your way around them. Information hunts that involve choosing a suitable book, using the contents page, index and subheadings, looking for topic sentences (usually the first in each paragraph) and scanning for key words are helpful.

Identifying main points is more sophisticated – you are trying to follow the writer's agenda rather than, as with information hunts, following your own.

HELPING CHILDREN IDENTIFY THE MAIN POINTS

Reading for information is different from reading a story. You can help children grasp the main points by:

✧ reading a passage aloud to the children and then asking them to note down the main points as you re-read it. You may tell them, 'There are three main points about looking after pets. Just write down one or two words to remind you.' Follow this up with a discussion of the main points they identified;

✧ giving the children a paragraph to read and asking them to choose a suitable title for it;

✧ giving them a passage to read and asking them to underline what they think are the main points, but telling them they are only allowed a specific, limited number of underlinings (so they must prioritize).

The last two of these tasks are best undertaken initially as small group work, involving discussion and argument.

INTEGRATING INFORMATION INTO A SCHEMA

As we read, we forget the words and remember the meaning. This meaning is compounded of the literal, and the inferences and elaborations we have made while reading. Making inferences is part of reading work, and it takes measurable time (microseconds!). The more such work the child puts into reading, the better she is able to remember the gist. This is because she has created a more coherent and complete picture by marrying her pre-existing knowledge with the information in the text.

Children get better at making inferences and at remembering gists as they grow older and this is, in part, a result of more attentive reading work, making more inferences and connections, and, in part, a result of their having more and better structured background information to bring to the text. At the age of five or children can recall what was explicit in texts better than they can recall what was implied, but in the later primary years they recall the explicit and the inferred in an integrated way.

SELF-MONITORING COMPREHENSION

Young children often do not realize when they don't understand something or when something doesn't make sense. One reason may be that they think of reading as being about decoding, and not about making sense. Or they read so slowly, they don't always follow the syntax, but read in a word-by-word way.

Another reason may be because they have insufficient knowledge and experience to see gaps or contradictions. Or it may be because they don't always (perhaps because of limitations in their working memories) make the inferences that might highlight the gaps or contradictions, and they don't always integrate the information in the text in a way that would show them up. For example, they may not see gaps in instructions until they try to carry them out. In reading the instructions, they haven't rehearsed them in imagination.

Children are generally aware when they don't understand a word, but less aware when they don't understand a sentence, still less a passage. In test situations young children have been shown not to be able to spot explicit inconsistencies and contradictions between adjacent sentences:

> ... An ant must have a nose in order to smell this chemical odor. Another thing about ants is that they do not have a nose. Ants cannot smell this odor. Ants can always find their way home by smelling this odor to follow the trail.
>
> (quoted in Oakhill and Garnham, 1988, page 116)

It is as if they are dealing with sentences one at a time, and if they can understand each sentence separately, this satisfies them. They have not integrated the information. Clearly it is important to know when one doesn't understand or hasn't enough information on a topic, so one can seek further enlightenment.

Fortunately, time and experience and focused teaching can do a lot about this. If children are told to look for contradictions in the passage, they tend to spot them!

PROMOTING SELF-MONITORING OF COMPREHENSION

✧ Jokes and nonsense poetry can be used to alert children to spotting inconsistencies and implausibilities at a certain level. Children's jokes often draw attention to linguistic ambiguities. Nonsense poetry often conjures up impossible or implausible images.

✧ Encourage children to notice and note words that they don't understand, even to the extent of making a class dictionary with individually signed entries. Similarly, praise children who ask you about things they don't understand – 'I'm glad you asked that. It's good that you want to understand. Well done.'

✧ Give children a 'doctored' text with irrelevant, inconsistent or nonsensical sentences interpolated, and then ask them what should be crossed out to make the passage make sense. This task is best done as a group activity in order to promote discussion.

✧ In researching a topic, ask them to list the questions they would like answered. This both gets them to review their existing knowledge and its gaps, and to approach their reading in a focused way. Also ask them to record things they found out that surprised or interested them; and to record any things they didn't understand or want further information about.

TEACHING COMPREHENSION

All the comprehension skills we have discussed occur spontaneously in children to some degree, so the teacher's task is to develop and extend something that comes naturally. It is also fortunate, as far as teaching is concerned, that oral comprehension and reading comprehension are fundamentally the same thing. What makes reading comprehension more problematic for some children is not the comprehension but the reading!

We can, therefore, engage children in oral comprehension work that will benefit their reading comprehension. At first, perhaps, we simply tell or read them stories. But it is also valuable to read information books aloud to children. History books that tend to chronological writing and narrative might be a useful place to start. But science books also deserve their place – especially if you think that the book explains certain things better than you could do yourself!

So rather than designing comprehension tests which are usually pretty deadly, why not consider the following?

Telling (rather than reading) stories. You might find this scary at first, but once you get into it, it is great fun. Among the advantages are that you can watch the children all the time, make eye contact with individuals and gather them in with minimum disruption. You can be alert to wandering attention and whether the children are following the story and adapt the story to the children as you go along. As far as teaching comprehension goes, the great advantage is that you can engage the children's attention through the storyteller's techniques of asking questions like, 'How do you think they could get home?', 'What had Hansel been doing all the way through the woods?', 'Oh, but what do you think happened to the crumbs that Hansel had dropped?', 'What do you think would happen to crumbs if you dropped them outside?'

With techniques of this kind you can remind the children what happened earlier and its significance now – you are getting the children to furnish the story from their own experience and imagination, you are encouraging them to anticipate and feel suspense. You are helping them to savour the shaping of the story. All this is comprehension.

Reading stories aloud to children. At the most basic comprehension level, this teaches children what books and print are for and that the wording is always the same, however many times you read the book. It gives children experience of literary language and of new grammatical usages which you mediate to them by your fluent intonation. It offers children access to a wider range of literary experience than they might cope with on their own.

Reading longer stories and serials increases children's attention span as the plot develops across time. With serial stories, you can recap by asking questions in order, not only to remind the children of what happened last time, but also to excite anticipation of what might happen next. What situations and issues were left hanging fire? It should be a reminder of the whole shaping of the narrative up to this point.

Reading information texts aloud should raise interest and

curiosity or provide answers to the questions that the children have raised or been alerted to about an ongoing topic. Before reading, you should explain to the children that you will be expecting them to raise or be able to answer questions about it afterwards – that is, you provide them with a focus for listening. After the reading, go through the topic questions, prompting the children to offer elaborated answers – 'Can you tell me more? Why would that be?' After this, the children should then review what they have learned. Have they got all the information they need? Did they learn anything new that they hadn't expected? Do they need to review the text to clear anything up? You may re-read the passage or leave the book available for consultation. In this way, your approach is a way of modelling information skills with the children.

CONCLUSION

The aim of reading is to understand what has been written. But understanding needs to operate at more than a literal level. The reader has to fill out the meaning by making inferences and elaborating the picture from her own experience and knowledge. With stories, the reader should respond to the characters with empathy and have a moral alertness to situations.

Beyond 'living the story', the reader has to stand back from it, understand the different characters' viewpoints and evaluate their behaviour. And beyond even this, the reader has to relate the experience of the story with her own experience to decide whether the story is credible and enjoyable, and whether it throws light on her own experiences, behaviour and values.

These skills do not come all at once, but it is the teacher's task to move the children in their direction. With any particular story, different aspects of comprehension emerge at different points in reading it. Some of the more evaluative elements only tend to crystallize *after* the story has been finished and reflected on – often only during discussion.

CHAPTER 11

LISTENING TO READERS

Listening to readers provides very specific opportunities both for diagnostic assessment and for individual teaching. This chapter begins by looking at the diagnostic assessment of reading skills using miscue analysis and suggests specific ways of prompting the development of children's reading strategies both while they are reading and later through direct class or group teaching. The skills the teacher learns through doing miscue analyses are invaluable in day-to-day teaching.

MISCUE ANALYSIS AND RUNNING RECORDS

Both miscue analysis (developed by Ken Goodman) and running records (developed by Marie Clay) involve recording children's responses verbatim when reading continuous text. While Goodman suggests using a text that challenges the child in order to secure enough miscues to analyse, Clay suggests using texts at three levels: one, at the child's current level, and then one each at an easier and a harder level. This is to get a more all-round view of the child as reader.

From responses recorded verbatim you are able to interpret the mistakes and thus understand how the child is trying to tackle the task of reading. Goodman (1967) prefers the term 'miscue' to 'mistake' because 'miscue' gives the child credit for trying to respond to some 'cue' (or clue) in the text. Goodman (1973) argues that when we understand what children are trying to do, their miscues open a window onto their reading strategies. (See the Appendix for details about miscue analysis.)

Good reading progress will be characterized by the child using or attempting to use all three sources of information:

✧ *graphophonics* – attending to the print and decoding;

✧ *syntax* – sensitivity to the grammatical demands within the sentence;

✧ *semantics* – attentiveness to the meaning of what is being read.

Not only will the child use all three sources but, hopefully, she will use them together, coordinating information from all three. One sign of this coordination is readiness to self-correct – to go back spontaneously after a miscue and re-read the word or phrase correctly.

Self-correction means the child has been self-monitoring and cross-checking between the sources of information. This may result from the child's using meaning 'as a checking device' (as it says in the National Curriculum) and noticing something doesn't make sense. Or it may be that the child notices a mismatch between what she has said and the word on the page.

INTERPRETING MISCUES

Before we look at scoring miscue analyses, let us look at some specific miscues – because the value of any scores depends on getting the interpretation of particular miscues right.

If a child misreads a word, there will be a reason for it, or even a number of reasons! Let us consider this miscue from Daniel (Year 3):

> Pete's mum kissed him at the Longdale Park Junior School
> gate. Pete hopened nobody was looking.

Semantically, Daniel's 'hopened' was suggested by the word 'gate' – the context has primed him to expect something relating to gates and going through them. Graphophonically, he has partially processed 'hoped' and the sound (or spelling) has triggered a response that relates to the contextual expectation. Syntactically, 'Pete' is likely to be followed by a verb, and the word that follows has an '-ed' ending – so a verb is what Daniel supplies. Thus we can see that semantic, graphophonic and syntactic cues have all contributed to this miscue.

Clearly, if he had fully processed the spelling, there would have been no miscue. But granted a miscue occurred, what further strategic shortfalls are present? Daniel has not used meaning *as a checking device*: neither the word nor the sentence makes sense. Without such checking for meaning, the mistake cannot be detected and corrected.

Cross-checking between different sources of information and self-correcting as necessary are absolutely vital for balanced reading development. Self-correction constitutes a form of self-tutoring, leading to more skilful reading – but it depends on attentive self-monitoring. So self-monitoring and self-correction are behaviours that the teacher must encourage.

How can one do this? In this particular instance, the teacher might interrupt the reading at the bottom of the page and say to Daniel, 'You read that page very nicely, but there was one bit that didn't make sense. Can you show me the sentence that didn't make sense?'

In general, Daniel is already fairly good at self-monitoring – he self-corrects roughly one in three miscues, which is a good ratio. For example, he tried 'sled', 'sleeped' and 'sled' again, before correctly reading 'slipped'. Whether it was meaning or the mismatch with the printed word that alerted him, we cannot tell. Indeed, had he tried the word silently rather than aloud, we would probably only have recorded a hesitation, not a self-corrected miscue!

But he still sometimes needs prompting to check for meaning and to work it through to success. Despite a number of tries, he could not get beyond producing, '... no matter hoe hand he tried' when the text said '... no matter how hard he tried'.

It seemed as if his graphophonics let him down – he couldn't process 'how' as sounding like 'cow' rather than 'low'. And having missed out on the grammar of the phrase beginning with 'how', he had no syntactic cue to help him with 'hard'. In a context to do with tying ties, 'hand' suggested itself – and 'hoe hand' doesn't make any less sense than 'hoe hard'!

Daniel appeared unhappy that the sentence didn't make sense, but clearly this was not enough. What he needed was a strategy for tackling problems with meaning by reviewing the graphophonics more analytically. The teacher could orientate him by saying, 'You weren't happy with that sentence, were you? Was it because it didn't make sense? Where did it go wrong?'

She could then prompt him to search his knowledge about '-ow' words and so on. For example, the teacher could ask him to read 'slow' and 'cow' before trying 'how' again and then re-reading the whole sentence.

In this way the teacher models self-correcting strategies for the child. In many ways such modelling is simply a matter of reminding the child of what she already knows. But what is new to the child is learning how to use that knowledge strategically to solve a problem.

INTERPRETING A MISCUE ANALYSIS

Let us now look at the overall miscue analysis for Daniel (shown overleaf). The book used was *No Worries* (Collins *Pathways*). In this analysis I have not distinguished between all the different type of miscues, but what I have done is use Goodman's distinction between 'good' and 'bad' miscues, where a 'good' miscue is one that makes sense in context, and a 'bad' miscue is one that turns the reading into nonsense.

The pattern of overlapping circles represents the contributions of the different sources of information to any particular miscue – thus, when Daniel read, 'She telled it for him' for 'She tied it for him', the dot representing this miscue appears in the overlap between graphophonics and syntax, since he has used the 't...ed' from graphophonics as a cue; and the substitution is a verb, as required by the syntax. But the dot is outside the semantic circle because the substitution doesn't make sense. Where Daniel read 'card' for 'cried', the dot representing this miscue falls in the graphophonic circle but outside the syntactic and semantic circles because this substitution, though prompted by graphophonic cues, makes neither syntactic nor semantic sense.

This graphic representation of miscues gives a quick impression of how far the child is exploiting any particular source of information.

DANIEL YR 3 405 WORDS

Miscues:

Self-corrections 14

'Good' miscues 12

'Bad' miscues 19

USE OF SOURCES OF INFORMATION

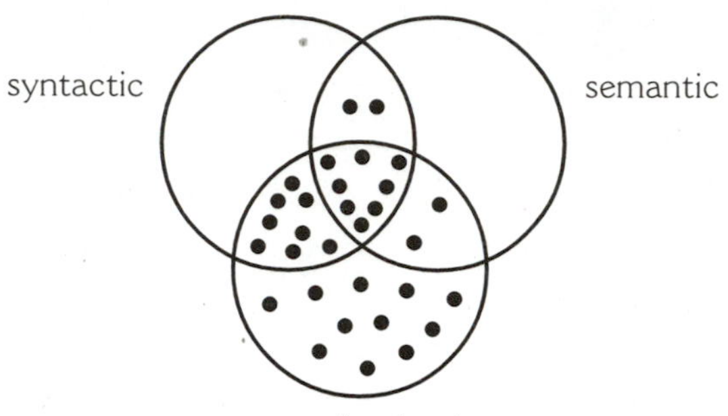

Even if a child is producing miscues, one would hope that he or she is trying to use and coordinate all the sources of information. So the more dots in the central overlap the better. And the fewer resulting from the use of only one source the better. What is clear is that Daniel doesn't simply guess on the basis of meaning, nor respond on the basis only of syntax (which in any event would be unusual). But he does sometimes operate on the basis only of graphophonics. This means, of course, on the basis of half-processed graphophonics (because otherwise there'd be no miscue!). He perhaps needs to be helped both to process his graphophonics better and to cross-check the graphophonic outcome with the context. The 'comprehending' score given below suggests the same sort of thing.

SELF-CORRECTION RATIO

self-corrections: (miscues + self-corrections) = 14:45 = 1:3.2

Marie Clay reckons a ratio of 1:3–5 is good; 1:20 is poor.

Lack of self-correction is a danger sign. Daniel's self-correction rate is good. It seems he is self-monitoring well enough to learn more about reading from reading. Self-correction indicates self-monitoring and hence, hopefully, self-tutoring. (But see below...).

ACCURACY:

$$100 - \left(\frac{\text{total no. of miscues} \times 100}{\text{total no. of words in text}}\right) = 100 - \left(\frac{31 \times 100}{405}\right) = 92.3\%$$

Marie Clay believes that 90–95% accuracy is needed for children to be able to benefit from their reading. There is just enough 'stretch' in this material to benefit Daniel – if his self-teaching strategies are effective.

'COMPREHENDING' SCORE (A MEASURE OF 'GOODNESS' OF MISCUES):

$$\frac{\text{'good' + corrected 'bad' miscues}}{\text{total miscues}} \times 100 = \frac{12+14 \times 100}{45} = 58\%$$

This means he tolerates (or doesn't notice) more than 40% of his miscues not making sense. As we have already suggested, he might be challenged about such instances at the end of the page.

COMPREHENSION

Daniel's comprehension was fine and he gave his answers in whole sentences, suggesting that the information was well-organized and integrated.

There are other analyses that can be done, but these are the ones that interest me most. The Venn diagram gives an indication of the balance between the three sources of information. The 'comprehending' score does not measure comprehension, but it does suggest how far the child is concerned with whether the text is making sense. The accuracy score shows how far the reading is under the control of print. The self-correction ratio suggests how far the child is self-monitoring and hence self-tutoring and, therefore, how well equipped he or she is to 'learn to read by reading'.

The information gained from the analysis needs to be interpreted in terms of both the child you know and your understanding of how reading development progresses. The result may be to suggest remedial or supportive lines of action.

Though Daniel tends to score quite well, his performance throws up certain issues. He uses repetition for a number of different purposes:

✧ dissatisfied repetition, for example, as with 'hoe hand', almost as if desperately hoping for inspiration;

✧ confident repetition, in order to recap and move on with fluency once a problem has been solved;

✧ time-filling repetition, as a substitute for hesitation while working out what comes next;

✧ first syllable repetition, while working out the rest of the word, for example, man...manage, to...together, no...nobody;

✧ onset repetition, to hear how it sounds, hoping this may prompt recognition, for example, fr...friend, g...gate.

These last two types show sensitivity to graphic chunking and to onsets. Repetition for fluency shows him to be putting the meaning together in syntactic chunks. Unconvinced repetition shows that he is monitoring his own understanding but hasn't solved the problem.

His attempts to solve problems often take the form of trying to exploit contextual meanings. Where Pete, in the story, is repeating the instructions for tying the knot in his tie to himself, the text says, 'He said over and over...', but Daniel read, 'He side over... side over...'. Then for 'Right side over and round twice', he said, 'Right said over and round twiss'. It is as if he was so anticipating the meaning, he got the word 'side' in too early and confuses himself, and he transformed 'twice' in the direction of 'twist'. Further on, when Pete finds yellow paint on a blazer, the text says, 'The blazer was Kulbir's!' But, falling between the two stools of graphophonics and meaning, Daniel read, 'The blazer was cluv... covered... clovered.' His contextual guesses got him into all kinds of problems, trying to reassemble the letter sounds in 'Kulbir' into something closer to his prediction!

Sometimes the analysis throws up quite specific points, like Daniel's tendency to say 'card' for any single syllable word beginning with 'ca-'. Maybe this highlights a more general point, that he is, to some extent, stuck at the pre- or partial alphabetic stage, and doesn't analyse the whole spelling patterns of words: for example, he reads 'priestly' for 'perfectly' and 'paint' for 'panic'. In a story that is about tying a knot in a tie, he stumbles again and again over the word 'knot' (variously, 'note', 'nought') and the words 'tie' and 'tied' ('tay', 'telled'), despite getting them right sometimes. He doesn't have an effective graphophonic system for analysing a spelling and learning it. Certain words he tackles anew each time he meets them, as if he had never succeeded with them before.

Daniel's contextual guessing is sometimes more of a hindrance than a help. But the more critical point seems to be a weakness in his graphophonic processing. Without developing this as a strategy when encountering problem words, he's going to go on bumbling through, failing to learn as much as he might from his reading. He will neither succeed in working words out very well, nor remembering those he has encountered because he won't have worked out a mental spelling template or recognition unit for them.

The conclusions I would want to append to Daniel's miscue analysis notes would be:

> The text was at the right sort of level for Daniel who is progressing fairly satisfactorily, but he needs to be encouraged to monitor for meaning more thoroughly and to tackle problems by developing more thoroughgoing graphophonic strategies. He might repay help with analysing spellings, graphophonic chunking and so on.

HELPING READERS WITH READING

We need strategies to help readers *while* they are reading, and we need to consider activities to undertake at other times, perhaps during the Literacy Hour, that will *feed into* reading. For example, Daniel could be prompted with questions like, 'Did that make sense?' and 'Look at that word again. Now go back and re-read the sentence'. But in addition he might profit from activities that make him look more analytically at spellings, especially at the second half of words, at rimes.

HELP WHILE READING

In the Introduction and earlier in this chapter, we touched on a number of prompting strategies. Here we will try to draw some of these points together. Depending on the problem, we might want to say:

✧ (if the child is losing her way and omitting words or guessing) 'Point to each word as you say it.'

✧ (if a child is stuck) 'Sound the first letter.'

✧ (if the problem word is regular) 'Try sounding out the letters.'

✧ (to prompt guessing and checking, cover the word) 'What do you think it might say? What would that begin with? What would you see at the end? Let's see. Were you right? How do you know?'

✧ (for a misread word) 'Try that again' (or, for a phrase or sentence) 'Try that again from the beginning.'

✧ (for a misread word, encouraging cross-checking against spelling) 'Does it start like that?'

✧ (if the child is stuck on a complex word, cover part of it, showing the stem, a key syllable, onset or rime, and thus build up the word) 'Look at that bit. What does it say? Right. Now look at it with this bit added…'

✧ (if the child has misread a word and made nonsense) 'Does that make sense? Which word do you think you got wrong?'

✧ (after a struggle) 'I liked the way you did that. You found the hard bit. Where was it? What made it hard?'

✧ (after a valiant attempt) 'Well done. You tried really hard to work it out. What makes it hard?'

✧ (after a 'good' miscue) 'It could be... But look... Check to see if it looks/sounds right.'

✧ (after a pause while a child works it out) 'That was good. You tried to work it out for yourself. How did you do it? How did you know it said...?'

✧ (after working out a word or being helped with it) 'Look at it carefully. Do you think you will know it another time?'

✧ (at the end of a page where the child made a mistake) 'I liked the way you read that. But you made a mistake on that page. Can you show me where? What was wrong?'

Prompts like these, as well as developing particular strategies, encourage self-monitoring reflectiveness. They encourage the child to feel she can work things out and that it will make sense.

ACTIVITIES THAT FEED INTO READING

These activities can be grouped according to the source of information they focus on.

SEMANTIC FOCUS

Children can be helped to seek meaning in texts through both listening and reading. (See Chapter 10 for a fuller discussion.) Activities might include:

✧ listening to stories and discussing inferential questions, mental images, responses, related personal experiences and so on;

✧ listening to, or reading, texts to get particular information, such as answers to prior questions;

✧ reading instructions or recipes and carrying out procedures;

✧ preparing a passage for reading aloud with the explicit aim of achieving fluency;

✧ retelling a story in the child's own words;

✧ shared reading and discussion of stories, poems, information texts;

✧ giving titles to stories, passages, poems;
✧ cloze procedures – words or sentences left blank;
✧ matching broken sentence halves to make sense;
✧ putting disordered sentences (or paragraphs) back into a meaningful sequence;
✧ discussing with the teacher books that have been read;
✧ writing book reviews, book promotion posters – possibly as shared tasks to involve discussion.

DEVELOPING SYNTACTIC AWARENESS

As teachers we are not always alert to the problems children have in making sense of the grammar of what they are reading, and we tend to treat their problems as purely graphophonic or semantic. (See Chapter 9 for a fuller discussion.) Consider, for example, Daniel's 'hoe hand' problem. It is unlikely he would have had a problem with 'hard' if he hadn't lost track of the grammar with 'hoe'.

The aim of developing syntactic awareness is not so much to develop conscious reflection as intuitive understanding. Since syntactic and semantic understandings operate so closely together, children are best introduced to new grammatical constructions and usages in contexts where the meaning helps their syntactic understanding. Many of these activities are best undertaken, initially, in small groups with the teacher to guide discussion:

✧ listening to stories written in a more literary idiom, in which the flow of the story makes the more complex or unusual language self-explanatory;
✧ listening to or reading a text, identifying unusual expressions and retelling the sense in the child's own words;
✧ sentence completion and cloze procedures with particular parts of speech or inflections deleted, for example, 'Jamie... the wall and jumped down... the garden... he saw... own bike... against the shed.'
✧ completing word inflections in sentences, for example, 'He like... to go fish...', 'She asked all ... friend.... to her party.'

✧ making and breaking complex sentences, for example, 'I was in town. I bought a video' can be transformed into 'When I was in town, I bought a video' or 'When in town, I bought a video' or even, 'In town, I bought a video'. (Ellipses (abbreviated grammar), as in the last two versions, are particularly difficult for children to grasp).

✧ completing cohesion between sentences and clauses, for example, 'It was Gemma's birthday. ... was very excited ... she was not going to have a party.'

DEVELOPING GRAPHOPHONIC SKILLS

See Chapters 5, 7 and 8 for a fuller discussion and for activities that can be used in the Literacy Hour. What follows are simply reminders:

✧ checking letter name knowledge and directionality, perhaps by getting children to spell out written words aloud;

✧ checking phonic knowledge, possibly by sounding out words or reading invented words;

✧ initial letter sound games, for example, variants to 'I spy' such as 'I hear with my little ear' and so on.

✧ rhyme and rime recognition activities, using clue-words, onset-rime dominoes, word families and so on.

✧ stems and affixes, perhaps deriving as many words as possible from a given stem, breaking complex words into morphemic chunks;

✧ breaking words into spelling sequences, for example, end blends, vowel digraphs, and finding companion words;

✧ word searches, for seeing spelling patterns as a whole.

EVERYDAY LISTENING TO READERS

You should aim to listen intensively to each child on a regular basis (adapted to the children's differing requirements) and to keep analytic records. With a child who has reached some level of reading independence, it is more appropriate, perhaps, to spend time discussing what has been read, what she has noticed about her own skills and difficulties, what she enjoys and would like to read next. The emphasis will fall more on self-monitoring and comprehension than on decoding. With other children, the emphasis falls more on diagnosis and supporting developing strategies.

Some writers suggest doing miscue analyses for each child twice a term, but twice a year would be more realistic! Doing them focuses very special attention on a child – and does a lot for your diagnostic sensitivity as well! It is not just for 'problem' cases. Daniel hardly constitutes a 'problem', yet without the focus gained by the analysis, it would be easy to miss his need for sharper graphophonic skills.

Don't forget that classroom helpers and parents can also listen to readers, and offering them some strategies for listening and prompting will be useful, for example, allowing the child time to work it out, re-reading up to the difficulty, questioning if something makes sense, or whether the text confirms the reading, prompting and praising (the easiest thing to forget!). But do not expect helpers to be as diagnostically attentive as you, nor to have such a repertoire of prompting skills available. Do not hand over total responsibility for hearing a child read to a helper, or you might lose track!

CONCLUSION

Listening to reading should not only be a matter of monitoring progress through a scheme but should be diagnostic, assessing the development of strategies and the use and coordination of the three sources of information – most fundamentally, the graphophonic. Coordination shows itself in self-correction, a key marker of development. Diagnosis, however, is pointless without remedial action to guide the child forward. The teacher can achieve this through prompting the child appropriately while listening to him or her read, or by devising further activities to reinforce skills that feed into reading.

CHAPTER 12

ORCHESTRATING TEACHING

Reading is a complex activity involving many interacting skills. Some are general skills to do with language and comprehension, and some are peculiar to dealing with written text. The National Literacy Strategy *Framework for Teaching* places great emphasis on the need for children to be able to 'orchestrate a full range of reading cues (phonic, graphic, syntactic, contextual) to monitor their reading and correct their mistakes' when tackling a text.

These cues or strategies are the ones we are familiar with from considering miscue analysis. They fall under two general headings.

'TOP-DOWN' (SEMANTIC AND SYNTACTIC) STRATEGIES

✧ knowledge of context: the child uses both the general context and the context of developing meaning within the sentence to prime word recognition;

✧ grammatical knowledge: the child uses his or her intuitive ability to grasp how the sequence and forms of words relate to each other within the sentence, to anticipate how the sentence is going, to prime word recognition and to put the sentence together meaningfully.

'BOTTOM-UP' (GRAPHOPHONIC) STRATEGIES

✧ phonic (sound/spelling) skills: the child derives pronunciations, and hence identifies words, from the graphophonic translation of spellings;

✧ word recognition: the child exploits her sight vocabulary in order to identify words and their meanings;

✧ graphic knowledge: the child identifies word parts, in

particular morphemic word endings, in order both to reconstruct complex words from pronounceable and meaningful part-word units and to recognize their grammatical significance within the sentence.

The metaphor of 'orchestration' implies that all these strategies must play their parts in balance and harmony to achieve the overall aim, which is the comprehension of the text. None of them is dispensable.

ORCHESTRATING 'ORCHESTRATION'

Different texts make different strategic demands. For example, an easy and predictable text may be tackled largely in terms of word recognition and straightforward comprehension. But a more difficult text may require the application of phonic and graphic skills to decode new vocabulary. It may require the exploitation of a half-grasped sense of the semantic context, supported by the framework of the syntax, to prompt hypotheses about the meanings of new words (or new meanings of known words) and hence the overall meaning of the sentence. This is why, to keep an overall balance, we should encourage challenging reading at one end of the spectrum to develop semantic/syntactic and decoding strategies, and easier reading or re-reading at the other, to promote fluency, comprehension and self-confidence.

When teaching reading, we need to teach knowledge, skills and a sense of strategy (which is the appropriate application of skills). And just as children need to learn to orchestrate their strategies, so we, as teachers, need to orchestrate our teaching to achieve this goal.

PROMOTING 'ORCHESTRATION'

Adams (1990) concludes:

> ... the process of reading cannot be divided into key and support activities. All of its component knowledge and skills must work together within a single integrated and interdependent system. And it is in that way that they must

> be acquired as well... The teacher must understand *why* each activity is included... The teacher must understand how the activities fit together in rationale, dependence and independence, and priority.
>
> (page 423)

For teaching, the notion of 'orchestration' or 'working together' has both large scale and small scale implications. The large scale implications are to do with:

✧ ensuring comprehensive and sequenced coverage of all that is required (the Termly Objectives in the *Framework for Teaching* aim to ensure this);

✧ keeping all the balls in the air at once, for example, teaching phonological skills, the alphabet, and a pre-alphabetic sight vocabulary all at the same time, and making links between them;

✧ planning activities, so that what is taught is immediately reinforced by practice;

✧ balancing instruction with independent reading, enabling the child to develop the application of the strategies you are teaching in her own experience.

The small-scale implications are to do with your diagnostic alertness to what the children are attempting, or not attempting, and to do with the quality of your pedagogic response.

Thus, the large scale implications of orchestration are to do with planning, based on 'Framework' objectives and your judgement about what skills the children need explicit procedural instruction in. The small scale are to do with diagnostic alertness and clarity of explanation in individual teaching and with prompting children, while engaged in reading, into the flexible application of the strategies they are learning.

THE NATIONAL LITERACY STRATEGY *FRAMEWORK FOR TEACHING*

Since orchestration means the balanced and appropriate interaction of parts, we should be suspicious of approaches to teaching that are linear, programmed and straitjacketing. If there is a royal road to reading, it winds about rather than following a straight line. A better metaphor might be a river, rising from many springs, coming together and gathering force. The *Framework for Teaching* recognizes this in its proposals about planning for teaching.

It specifies that work should be structured at three levels: the word level, concerned with phonics, spelling and vocabulary; the sentence level, concerned with grammar and punctuation; and the text level, concerned with comprehension and composition. And these levels are to be taught in parallel. We need to develop on many fronts at once, and keep the fronts in communication with each other.

At the same time as specifying this categorization of objectives, the *Framework for Teaching* specifies a 'Literacy Hour' which is a dedicated daily period for direct instruction and directed practice. The Literacy Hour, however, is not the only allocation of time devoted to reading. Sustained independent reading, reading to the teacher, topic research, listening to stories and so on, are undertaken outside the hour. The teacher-directed instruction and instructional activities support and develop the literacy skills that are being practised and used elsewhere in the timetable.

The *Framework for Teaching*, in the Termly Objectives, provides details of *what* should be taught during the Literacy Hour for the whole primary phase. Indeed, the draft version of the *Framework* was very explicit in saying that the aim of specifying objectives was 'to relieve you of the burden of planning *what* you should teach in order to concentrate on planning *how* to teach it'. What is left for the teacher to work out is how to achieve the balance and coverage of the objectives.

For efficiency, children are grouped by ability in order to permit differentiated work, and any particular group has about ten minutes of your undivided attention twice a week. If twenty minutes a day is devoted to group work and each group has twenty minutes direct teaching a week, this means five ability groups of approximately six children each. The *Framework* allows for a little variation in this structure to meet varying pupil needs but is insistent that the general balance as prescribed is maintained. This ensures that the structure and routines are clear and regular so that the time on-task is maximized and as little as possible is wasted on getting the children organized.

SELECTING GROUPS

Before going on to consider the Literacy Hour in detail, we should consider the criteria for selecting ability groups. What do we mean by 'ability' in this context? The answer has to be in terms of where the children are at and what they need to be taught next. For example, in Reception you will want to differentiate between those children who have a fair idea about how reading works and those who have no knowledge or experience of being read to. Their needs are different. More particularly, you will want to discriminate between children in terms of:

✧ which children listen attentively when you read to them, participate spontaneously in reading activities, choose and know how to look at books;

✧ how far different children seem to understand the conventions of print (directionality, one-to-one correspondence between written and spoken word, and so on);

✧ what phonological awareness they show through their enjoyment of and ability to produce rhymes and alliteration;

✧ what alphabetic knowledge and word recognition skills they bring with them.

Of these criteria, alphabetic knowledge and phonological awareness (in that order) are probably the most important because they are the best predictors of future reading success.

THE PATTERN OF THE LITERACY HOUR

The general pattern for the Literacy Hour is:

✧ 15 minutes whole-class reading session using a shared text, or a writing session on a collaborative writing task;

✧ 15 minutes whole-class session on word-level work at Key Stage 1, and on word-level or sentence-level work at Key Stage 2;

✧ 20 minutes directed group activities, with the teacher spending time equally between two groups on guided text work;

✧ 10 minutes whole-class work reviewing, reflecting on and consolidating teaching points and presenting work done in the lesson.

The Literacy Hour will clearly be divided between reading and writing, though this doesn't mean that each day the time has to be shared or shared equally. From here on, we will simply consider reading work.

DIRECT TEACHING

One of the aims of the *Framework* is to shift emphasis from bitty individualized help to structured and cohesive whole-class and group teaching. However, the model of direct teaching is not a chalk-and-talk 'transmission' model. The teaching style recommended is interactive, focused on text and what to do with it, with the children fully engaged and participating. The teacher will demonstrate and talk through procedures, explain and model skills applied to texts, probe and prompt children's understanding through open and leading questions, encourage children's oral participation and will listen and respond to their contributions. At the same time, the recommended style is purposeful, following the teacher's agenda, and alerting the children to the goals being striven for, so that they, too, will have a sense of purpose.

POSSIBLE TEACHING STRATEGIES

✧ *Explain what you want them to learn* by explicit teaching, for example, 'You can work out what a word says by sounding out the letters. Look: /p/, /a/, /t/. Can you hear what it says?' and so on.

✧ *Demonstrate the strategies* you want them to learn and talk them through as you do so. This is necessary, because you want them to learn not just the overt action (for example, picking up the book, looking at the back page), but the inward procedure and rationale ('The picture on the cover shows animals in a garden. The title says "Minibeasts at Home", so it could be the information book I want. So I'll look at the back cover to see what the blurb says... Right, now I'll look in the back of the book for the Index, so I can look up the page number for "spiders". First, I've got to find 'S'. 'O'. 'P'. 'Q'... 'S' comes a bit later'. Encourage them to talk themselves through their strategies in the tasks you provide.

✧ *Ask about the strategies the children are going to use* for a task. If, while the task is ongoing, they become stuck, ask them to explain what they are trying to do. If they have succeeded in solving a problem, ask them to tell you how they did it. Such explicitness on their part promotes planning, forethought and reflectivity.

✧ *Give them problems to solve* that require them to use the strategies that you have been talking about and demonstrating. It is a good idea to provide problems for groups to work on, and then to follow these up with individual problem solving. The group situation requires the children to discuss and be explicit about the strategies they are adopting. Individual work gives them individual responsibility and the chance to internalize the strategies.

✧ *Give them lots of practice* so that the strategies become habitual – and so that they become used to taking responsibility for trying to work things out for themselves.

✧ *Give help so that the child may succeed.* This doesn't mean solving the problem for the child, it means diagnosing the stumbling block, prompting perceptions and procedures or providing some information. Whatever you do, let it help the child to make the leap to the solution and enjoy that all-important, motivating Eureka! experience.

✧ *Give specific and positive feedback.* When giving praise, be specific about what it was you liked about the child's performance – 'I bet you feel good about reading your first book all by yourself,' or 'I loved the way I only had to say, "So what do you do next?", and you knew. You could do it by yourself!'

WHOLE-CLASS SHARED READING

Many of the objectives will be met during this activity. Careful selection of texts will ensure that the criteria about the range of reading materials – fiction, poetry and information texts – are met. The text provides the context for work at all three levels – word-level comprehension, sentence-level grammatical awareness and text-level work.

During the Reception Year, big books, or some other large-scale text, will provide a shared visual focus for the children, in terms of which you can establish things about the nature of books, print and directionality. By pointing to the words, you show that the print 'says' the words, that there is a one-to-one correspondence between the written and spoken word, that you read in a particular direction and that you can go back to check or re-read a certain part.

At the same time, you discuss the meaning of what is being read because one of the important things to demonstrate is that texts are there to get meanings from. By asking children on a first reading or a re-reading to anticipate and guess what words come next, you exercise the ability to predict, based upon an intuitive sense of meaning and grammar, and even, in the case of poetry, rhyme.

WHOLE-CLASS WORD WORK

At the earlier stages, in particular, word work will relate directly to the shared reading text. For example, the sight-words you are teaching will be ones found in the texts you are looking at. You may want the children to search the shared text to find particular sight-words or to identify particular letters. You may want to spend time looking at the spelling patterns of these words to help focus the attention of pre-alphabetic readers on the letters as the significant details to help identification. Many of the approaches discussed in the preceding chapters can be used, for example, teaching sight-words in the context of sentences from the shared reading text, teaching phonics and work on rhymes and their shared spelling patterns. These activities, for example, phonics, clue-word activities and so on, can subsequently be practised in group sessions. Whole-class writing sessions clearly give the opportunity for practising word-level work – 'What sound does the word "bring" begin with? Right. So what letter will we want to write?' Many phonological awareness activities can be undertaken as whole-class or taught-group activities.

TAUGHT-GROUP WORK

At Key Stage 1, the emphasis in group sessions should be on carefully guided reading, with particular attention paid to developing reading strategies and comprehension in the ways discussed in the previous two chapters. Taught-group work can be a very suitable situation for looking intensively at graphophonic skills – it gives good opportunities for close individual attention, especially as a follow-up to whole-class teaching. Other activities will include things like developing graphic knowledge through looking at inflections and agreements, or reading aloud with expression. Activities may be introduced here which groups are able to continue without assistance.

INDEPENDENT GROUP ACTIVITIES

While much of this time is likely to be devoted to writing, reading also has its place. Group reading without the teacher may begin with the more experienced readers in the later stages of Key Stage 1. It may follow on from a teacher-supported group reading session, and it could well be that this activity is based on the re-reading of a text the children have already tackled or which you have already read to them. Multiple texts are required. Give them an idea of how far you expect them to read and what questions you want them to consider. The children may read aloud in turn, read in pairs or read to themselves. Tackling problem words together, and the comprehension questions you have left them with, encourages group problem-solving and self-help.

Older children may simply be asked to read a poem together and discuss it – they can raise the questions that puzzle them and try to answer them together. A tape recorder can help to focus attention and you can focus discussion by asking them for a sentence or two to describe the poem or to choose a title for it. Or you might give them an advertisement to look at and ask them to list the things that the advertiser wants them to think, and list any questions they might want to ask about the product or service, or to use the text as a model for writing an advertisement for something that interests them.

Cloze passages (with selected words or a whole sentence replaced with a blank space) are good for promoting group discussion. The children need to work out the meaning in order to be able to fill in the blanks so that the passage makes sense.

Many of the activities in earlier chapters are appropriate for group work. Group discussion is a good way of getting children to become more explicit in the manner in which they think about a problem.

THE FINAL PLENARY TEN MINUTES

Plenary sessions with adults are notoriously unproductive, so it is important that you have a clear agenda for what you want the session to achieve. Your aim is to gather all the children in, clarify any issues that have arisen, celebrate what they have learned and accomplished in the lesson – especially problems they have solved and strategies they have successfully employed. In the process you will draw out of them their experiences of learning and you remind them of the goals of the lesson and what they have learned. You want them to reflect upon themselves as learners and to share your agenda for them. You want to get them to see themselves as successful learners in order to help them to be so!

READING OUTSIDE THE LITERACY HOUR

The notion of sustained independent reading has, to a very great extent, superseded the practice of 'reading to teacher' every day. This is not only because it is recognized that listening to readers is difficult to organize on a daily basis and that each child would only get a very short time allocation, but that, more positively, reading improves the more the child gets into it for longer periods and takes some responsibility for her own progress; and that teacher time is often better spent, with more able readers at least, discussing the story or conducting a 'reading conference' with the child about her reading.

While teacher-directed group reading gives the teacher a chance informally to hear how particular children are getting on, children will also need to be heard outside the Literacy Hour. As discussed earlier, all children should be heard for miscue analysis periodically (maybe twice a year), to get a more considered assessment of the balance and development of their reading strategies.

Some children will need to be heard more frequently than others. As these children are likely to be clustered in particular ability groups, your pattern of teaching different groups is likely to be different. Guided reading may well play a more prominent part in the work you do with some groups than others and you will need to find time outside the Literacy Hour to listen more frequently to these children.

ASSESSING READING

Miscue analysis provides periodic assessments of where children are at in developing and orchestrating their reading strategies. On a more regular basis, children's progress in the reading scheme gives some measure of their level of development. Objective reading tests can provide further evidence, but you are only likely to use these with any frequency when you are concerned by a child's lack of progress and feel the need for a measure that gives standardized results.

The most important assessments, however, are those you make daily from ongoing observations. Their quality and value depend upon the quality and criteria of your observations – which themselves depend upon your attentiveness and the underlying concepts you have about the reading process.

Assessment has two functions: one is to monitor and record development; the other is to inform your planning. In planning, assessment is where you start from. The whole teaching cycle goes like this:

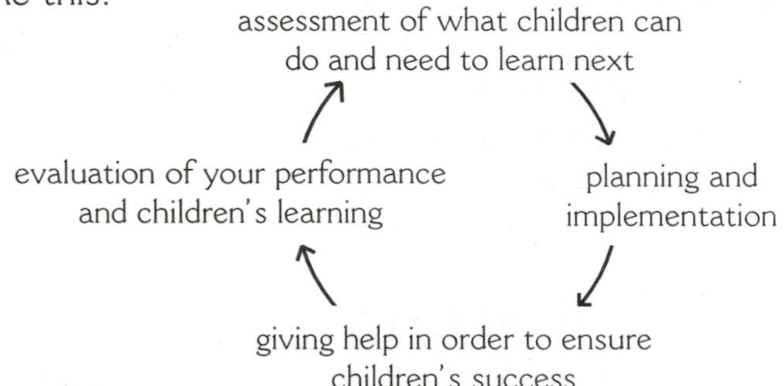

Since nothing succeeds like success, be alert to what children can do successfully in your assessments and evaluations, and praise them for it – even if it is only for trying. If they can't do something you have tried to teach, perhaps you should find another way of teaching it. If children can't answer a question, perhaps you have asked the wrong question! One crucial teaching skill is to design very small steps that children can be nudged into making successfully on their own.

CONCLUSION

Reading involves a complex collection of skills that all interact with, and act as checks and balances on each other. While, in the first instance, the skills may need to be taught separately, success depends upon how they operate together. Consequently our teaching needs to be an orchestrated juggling act, keeping many balls in the air at once and, more subtly than any juggling act, helping children to coordinate their various skills to identify the words and reconstruct the meanings in a text and, thus, to become self-developing readers.

APPENDIX

CARRYING OUT MISCUE ANALYSIS

PREPARATION

1. Select a passage of 100–200 words (perhaps the next step up in the reading scheme). You need two copies of the passage (it is best to remove pictures to avoid distractions).

2. Set up a tape recorder to record the session.

3. Prepare some questions, literal and inferential, to gain an impression of the child's comprehension.

ADMINISTERING

4. Explain to the child that the passage is a bit harder than usual because you are interested in how she manages and in the mistakes people make. Say you won't help unless she is really stuck. But not to worry! Let the child look at the passage for a few minutes before reading to you. If she makes no mistakes in the first 20 words or so, say 'You're too good!' and try something a little harder.

5. Record the reading and the subsequent comprehension discussion. You can let the child operate the recorder and afterwards listen to her own reading, telling you about it.

6. After the reading, ask your questions or ask the child to tell you what happened in the story to get a sense of her level of comprehension.

ANALYSING

7. Mark up your copy while the child is reading, or mark it up from the recording. (In any case, use the recording to check your marking-up.) You need at least 12–15 miscues for the analysis to be of any use.

8. Guide to coding miscues:

MISCUE TYPE	TEXT	RESPONSE	SYMBOL
substitution	shoulder	shouted	shouted ~~shoulder~~
omission	a big hug and a kiss	a big hug and kiss	a big hug and (a) kiss
insertion	Dad woke Kulbir	Dad woke up Kulbir	up Dad woke ^ Kulbir
reversal	...said Mum	...Mum said	...said Mum
self-correction	with Dad	when/with Dad	when✓ ~~with~~ Dad
hesitation	He blushed	He... blushed	He/blushed
repetition	was	was... was	was
sounding out	patted	p-a-tt-e-d	patted
refusal	yacht	(no attempt)	[yacht]

9. An example of marked-up text:

Pete took his blazer and walked home

haply side/sid
~~happily~~. He ~~said~~ over and over to himself,

said twiss
"Right ~~side~~ over and round ~~twice~~. Pull it
through to make a knot."

he✓ his
Halfway ~~home~~ Pete put ~~the~~ blazer on.
There was yellow paint on it! The blazer

cluv/covered/clovered
was ~~Kulbir's~~!

it paint pages
Pete ran back to school ~~in panic~~. The ~~pegs~~

where epty/eply
~~were empty~~.

INTERPRETING

10. Not all the 'miscues' you mark are strictly miscues. The miscues to be scored are any substitutions, insertions, omissions, reversals and refusals, if any.

11. See Chapter 11 for working out Venn diagrams, self-correction ratios, accuracy and 'comprehending' scores and for discussion of interpretation.

BIBLIOGRAPHY

Adams, M. J. (1990) *Beginning to Read: Thinking and Learning about Print*, Cambridge Mass., MIT Press

Beard, R. (ed.) (1993) *Teaching Literacy: Balancing Perspectives*, Hodder & Stoughton

Bielby, N. (1994) *Making Sense of Reading: The new phonics and its implications*, Scholastic

Brooks, G., Gorman, T., Kendal, L. and Tate, A. (1992) *What Teachers in Training are Taught about Reading*, NFER

Browne, A. (1996) *Developing Language and Literacy*, Chapman

Bryant, P. (1993) 'Phonological aspect of learning to read' in Beard, R. *Teaching Literacy: Balancing Perspectives*, Hodder & Stoughton

Bryant, P. and Bradley L. (1985) *Children's Reading Problems*, Blackwell

Bussis, A., Chittenden, E., Amarel, M. and Klausner, E. (1985) *Inquiry into Meaning*, Lawrence Erlbaum Associates

Byrne, B. (1998) *The Foundation of Literacy: the Child's Acquisition of the Alphabetic Principle*, Psychology Press

Carter, R. (ed) (1990) *Knowledge About Language and the Curriculum*, Hodder & Stoughton

Chall, J.S. (1983) *Learning to Read: The Great Debate* (revised edition), McGraw Hill

Chew, J. (1997) 'Traditional Phonics: What it is and what it is not' in the *Journal of Research in Reading*. Vol 20, No 3

Chomsky, C. (1979) 'Approaching Reading through Invented Spelling' in Resnick, L.B. and Weaver, P. A. (eds.) *Theory and Practice in Early Reading Volume 2*, Lawrence Erlbaum Associates

Chukovsky, K. (1963) *From Two to Five*, University of California

Clark, M.M. (1976) *Young Fluent Readers*, Heinemann

Clay, M.M. (1985) *The Early Detection of Reading Difficulties*, Heinemann

Clay, M.M. (1991) *Becoming Literate: The Construction of Inner Control*, Heinemann

Clay, M.M. (1993) *Reading Recovery: A Guide for Teachers in Training*, Heinemann

DFE (1995) *Key Stages 1 and 2 of the National Curriculum*, HMSO

DfEE (1998) *Framework for Teaching*, The National Literacy Strategy,HMSO

Downing, J. *Comparative Reading, Cross-National Studies of Behaviour and Processes in Reading and Writing*, Collier Macmillan

Ehri, L.C., Deffner, N. D. and Wilce, L. S. (1984) 'Pictorial mnemonics for phonics' in the *Journal of Educational Psychology*, Vol 76

Ehri, L.C. (1995) 'Phases of development in learning to read words by sight' in the *Journal of Research in Reading*, Vol 18, No 2

Elkonin, D.B. (1973) 'USSR' in Downing, J. *Comparative Reading: Cross-National Studies of Behaviour and Processes in Reading and Writing*, Collier Macmillan

Ellis, A.W. (1993) *Reading, Writing and Dyslexia: A Cognitive Analysis* (2nd edition), Lawrence Erlbaum Associates

Frith, U. (1985) 'Developmental Dyslexia' in Patterson, K.E. *et al*. (eds.) *Surface Dyslexia*, Lawrence Erlbaum Associates

Funnel, E. and Stuart, M. (eds.) (1995) *Learning to Read*, Blackwell

Gollasch, F.V. (ed.) (1982) *Language and Literacy: The Selected Writings of Kenneth S. Goodman*, Vol 1, Routledge and Kegan Paul

Goodman, K. (1967) 'Reading: A Psycholinguistic Guessing Game' in Gollasch F.V. (ed.) (1982) *Language and Literacy, The Selected Writings of Kenneth S. Goodman*, Vol 1, Routledge and Kegan Paul

Goodman, K. (1973) 'Miscues: Windows on the Reading Process' in Gollasch, F.V. (ed.) (1982) *Language and Literacy, The Selected Writings of Kenneth S. Goodman*, Vol 1, Routledge and Kegan Paul

Goswami, U. and Bryant, P. (1990) *Phonological Skills and Learning to Read*, Lawrence Erlbaum Associates

Goswami, U. (1993) 'Orthographic analogies and reading development' in *The Psychologist*, July 1993

Goswami, U. (1995) 'Phonological development and reading by analogy: What is analogy and what is not?' in the *Journal of Research in Reading* Vol 18, No 2

Goswami, U. (1996) *Rhyme and Analogy: Teacher's Guide* in the Oxford Reading Tree series, Oxford University Press

Goulandris, N. and Snowling, M. (1995) 'Assessing reading skills' in Funnel, E. and Stuart, M. *Learning to Read*, Blackwell

Harris, M. and Coltheart, M. (1990) *Language Processing in Children and Adults: An Introduction*, Routledge and Kegan Paul

Hatcher, P.J., Hulme, C. and Ellis, A. W. (1995) 'Helping to overcome early reading failure by combining the teaching of reading and phonological skills' in Funnel, E. and Stuart, M. *Learning to Read*, Blackwell

Iversen, S. and Turner, W.E. (1993) 'Phonological processing and the reading recovery programme' in the *Journal of Educational Psychology*, Vol 85

Iversen, S. (1997) *A Blueprint for Literacy Success*, Kingscourt

* *Fiction 2*, Longman Book Project, Longman Group

* Lutrario, Chris (1995) *The Magic Pencil*, Collins Pathways series, HarperCollins Publishers

McNally, J. and Murray, W. (1968) *Key Words to Literacy*, Schoolmaster Publishing

McNee, M. (1996) *Step by Step* (revised and enlarged), McNee

Meek, M. (1988) *How Texts Teach What Readers Learn*, Thimble Press

Meek, M. (1990) 'What Do We Know about Reading that Helps Us Teach?' in *Knowledge About Language and the Curriculum*, ed. Carter, R., Hodder & Stoughton

Nunes, T. (1998) *Developing children's minds through literacy and numeracy*, Institute of Education

Oakhill, J., Garnham, A. (1988) *Becoming a Skilled Reader*, Basil Blackwell

Oakhill, J. and Yuill, N. (1991) 'The Remediation of Reading Comprehension Difficulties' in Snowling, M. and Thomson, M. (eds.) *Dyslexia: Integrating Theory and Practice*, Whurr

Patterson, K.E., Marshall, J.C. and Coltheart, M. (1985) *Surface Dyslexia*, Lawrence Erlbaum Associates

Pinker, S. (1995) *The Language Instinct*, Penguin

Redfern, A. and Edwards V. (1992) *How Schools Teach Reading*, Reading and Language Education Centre

Resnick, L.B. and Weaver, P.A. (eds.) (1979) *Theory and Practice in Early Reading* ,Vol 2, Lawrence Erlbaum Associates

Seidenberg, M.S. and McClelland, J.L. (1989) 'A Distributed, Developmental Model of Word Recognition and Naming' in *Psychological Review*, Vol 96, No 4

Seymour, P.H.K. and Elder, L. (1985) 'Beginning Reading without Phonology' in *Cognitive Neuropsychology*, 1985

Slobin, D.I. (1978) *Studies in Child Language Development*, Holt, Rinehart and Winston

Smith, F. (1986) *Reading* (2nd edition), Cambridge University Press

Snowling, M. and Thomson, ME. (eds.) (1991) *Dyslexia: Integrating Theory and Practice*, Whurr

Story Chest, *Teacher's File* (1993), Nelson

Stuart, M. (1995) 'Recognising printed words unlocks the door to reading: How do children find the key?' in Funnel, E. and Stuart, M., *Learning to Read*, Blackwell

Taylor, I. and Olson, D.R. (eds.) (1997) *Scripts and Literacy: Reading and learning to read Alphabets, Syllabaries and Characters*, Kluwer

Turner, M. and Burkard, T. (1996) *Reading Fever: Why phonics must come first*, Centre for Policy Studies

Venezky, R.L. (1995) 'How English is read: Grapheme-phoneme regularity and orthographic structure in word recognition' in Taylor, I. and Olson, D.R. (eds.) (1997) *Scripts and Literacy: Reading and learning to read Alphabets, Syllabaries and Characters*, Kluwer

* Wade, B. and Moore, M. (1996) *The New Baby*, Collins Pathways series, HarperCollins Publishers

* Wade, B. and Moore, M. (1996) *No Worries*, Collins Pathways series, HarperCollins Publishers

* Wade, B. and Moore, M. (1996) *Sticks and Stones*, Collins Pathways series, HarperCollins Publishers

Note: the symbol * denotes a children's book.

INDEX